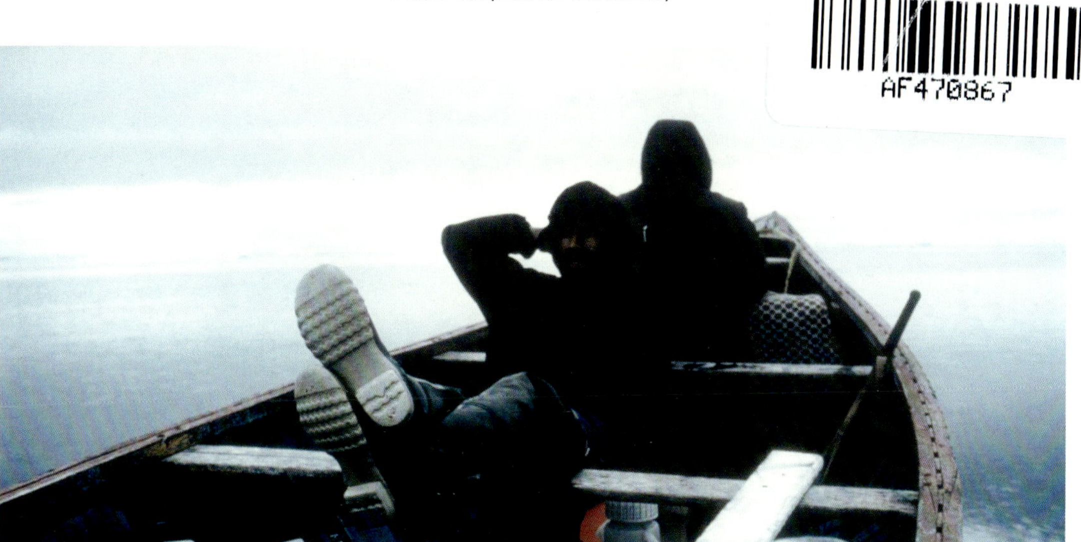

Plate 1
Simon Quassa from the Inuit Broadcasting Corporation relaxing with a ringed seal in
the foreground after a day of filming seals for a documentary, 1988.
Photo: Michael Bravo

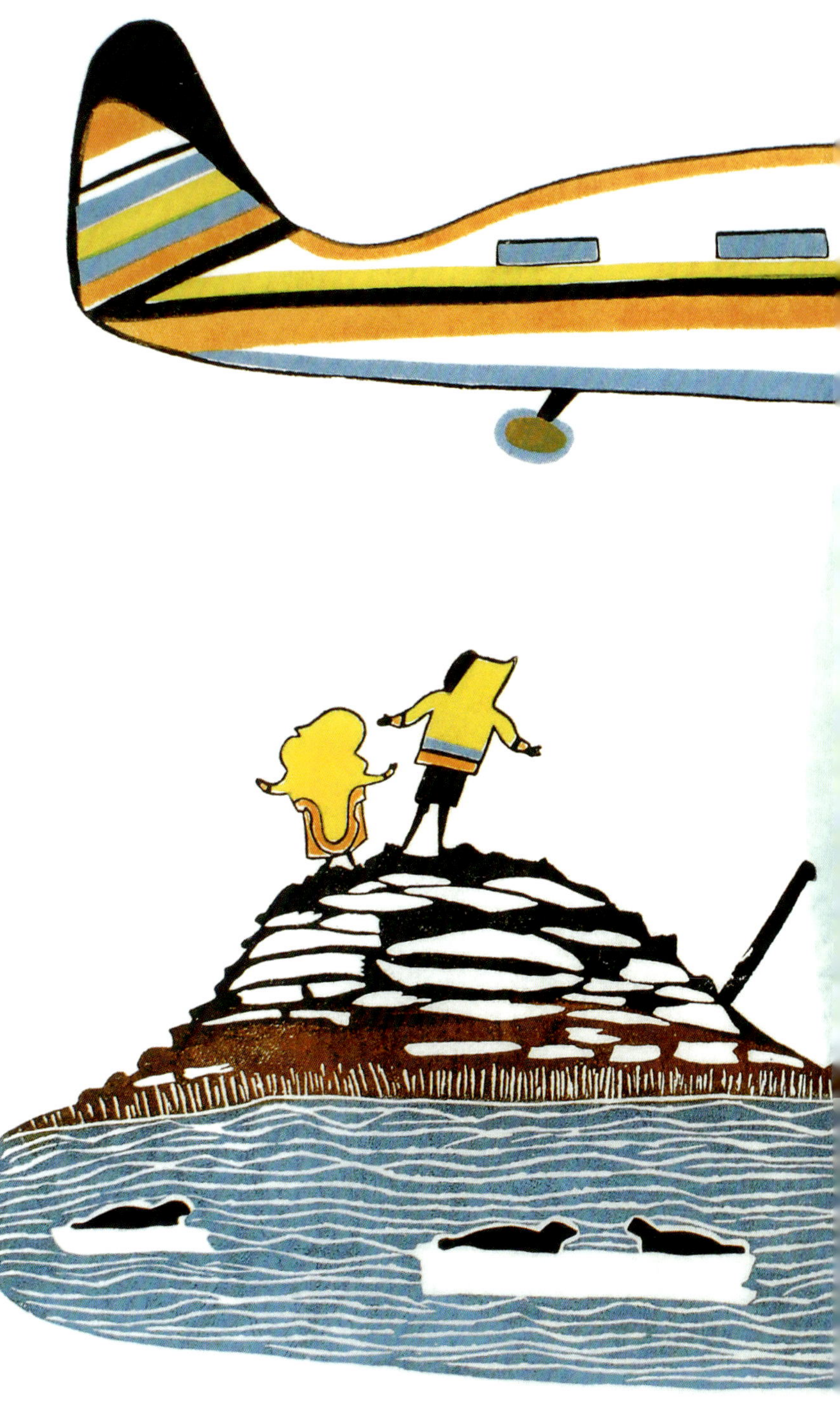

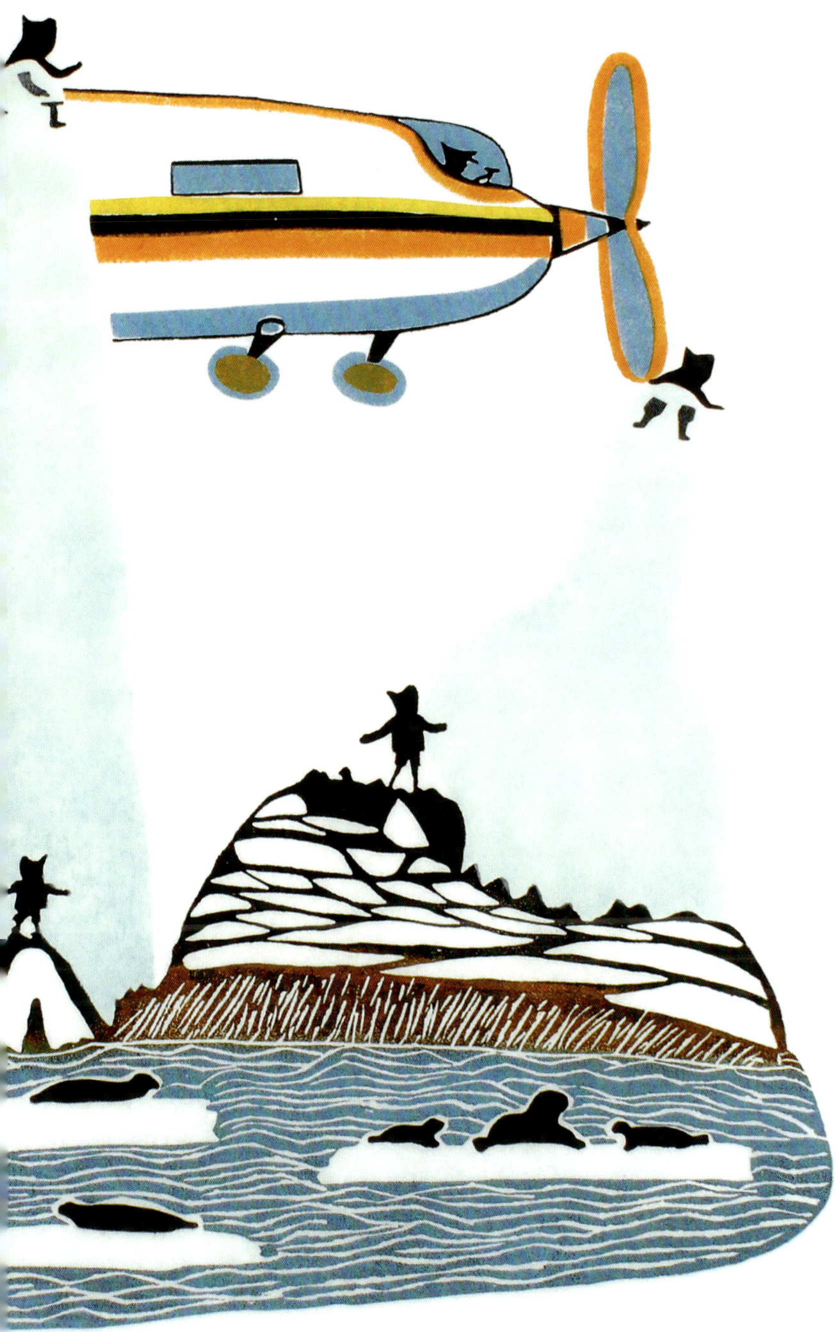

Plate 2
Pudlo Pudlat, *Aeroplane*, 1976.
Reproduced with the permission of Dorset Fine Arts

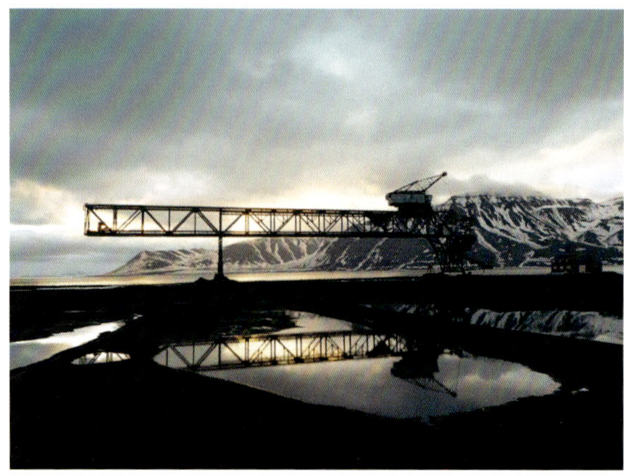

Plate 3
Nathalie Grenzhaeuser, *Hotellneset*, 2007, from the series
The Construction of the Quiet Earth. LightJet print, Diasec
matte, 120 x 160 cm, edition 5 & 2 AP

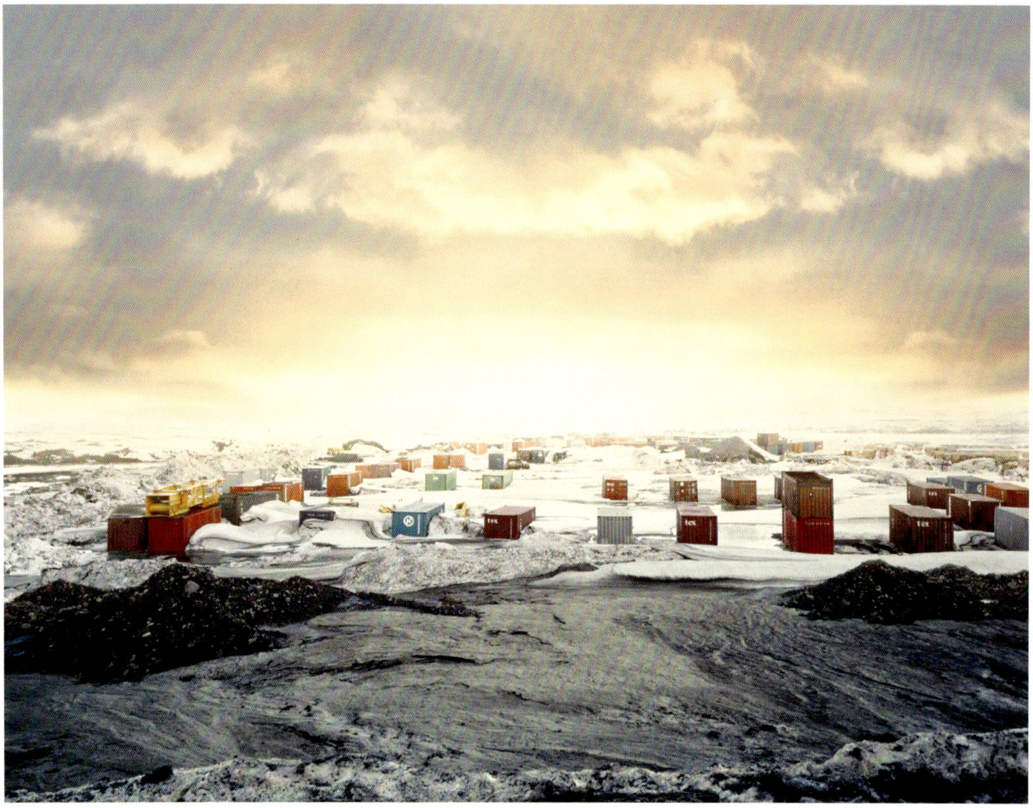

Plate 4
Nathalie Grenzhaeuser, *Kapp Amsterdam*, 2007, from the series *The Construction of
the Quiet Earth.* LightJet print, Diasec matte, 120 x 160 cm, edition 5 & 2 AP

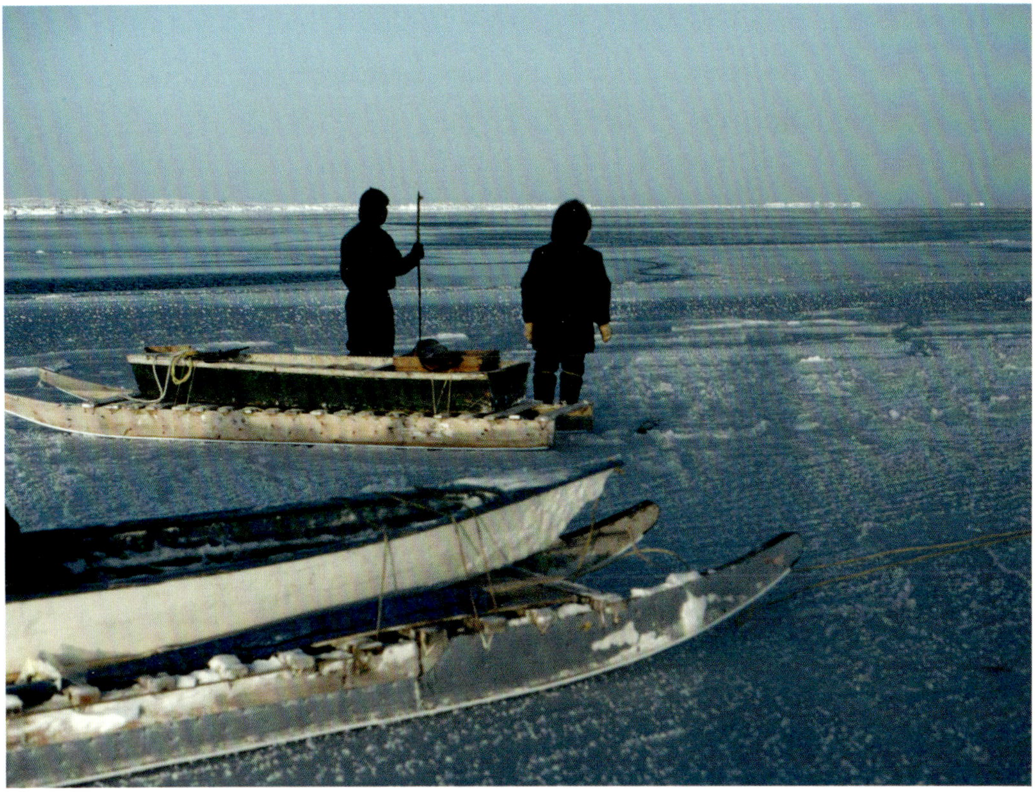

Plate 5
Hunters survey the sea ice off the coast of Igloolik, 1988.
Photo: Michael Bravo

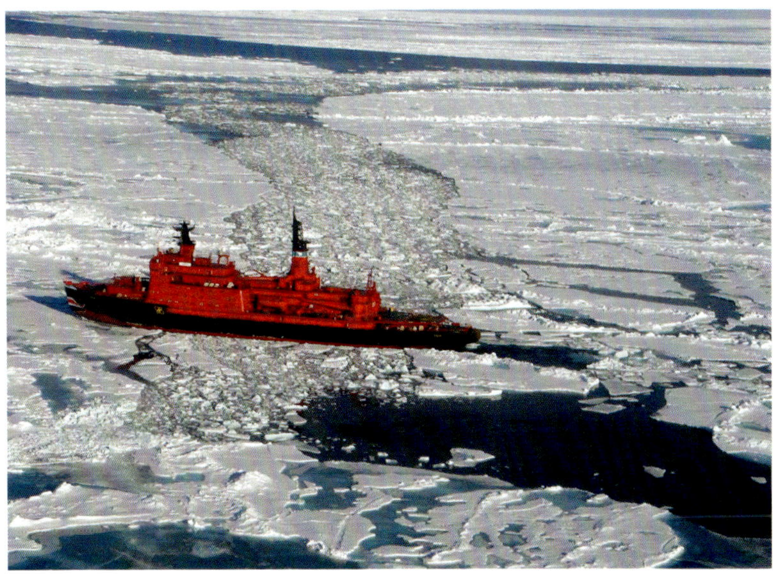

Plate 6
Nuclear icebreaker *Yamal* on its way to the North Pole carrying 100 tourists
Photo: Wofratz/Wikimedia Commons

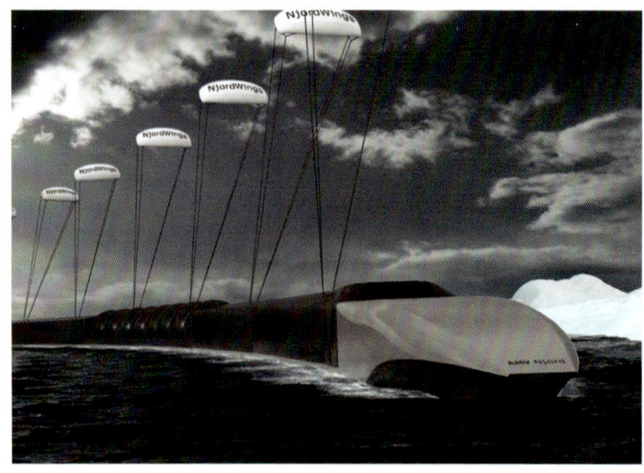

Plate 7
Green, modular, futuristic Arctic icebreaker concept from *Setting the Course: Sustainable Arctic Shipping,* Courtesy of DNV 2010.

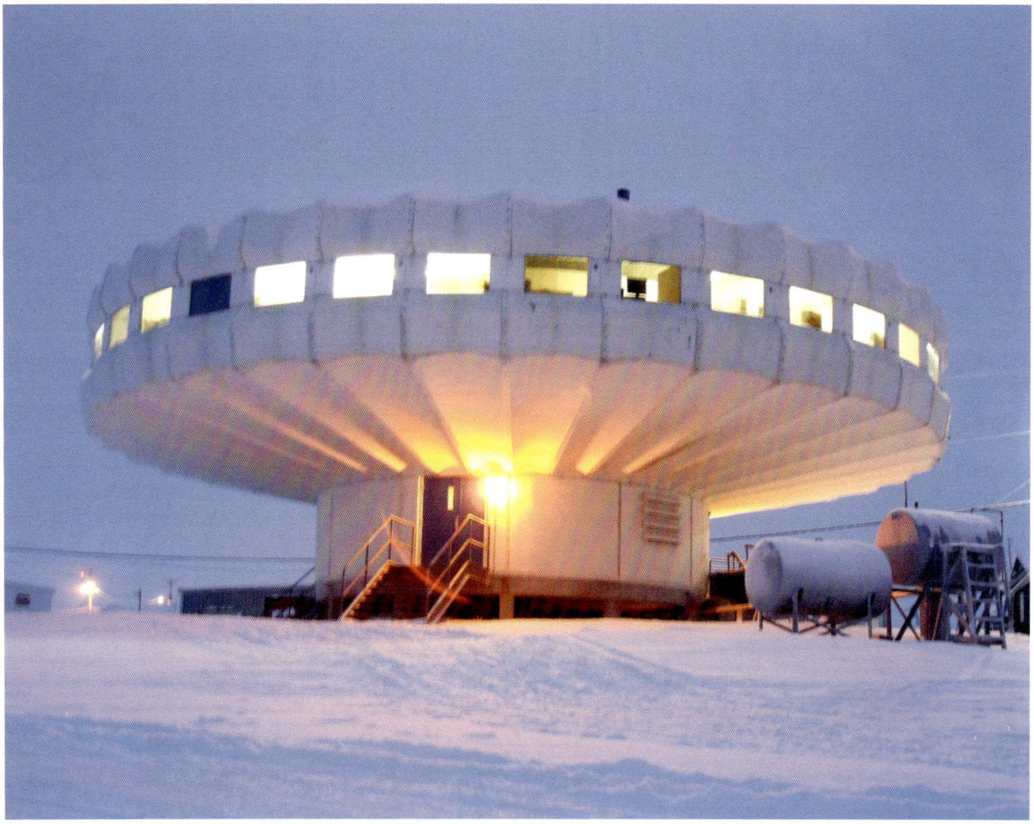

Plate 8
"The Lab," or Eastern Arctic Research Center, Igloolik, constructed in 1975. The effort to involve the community in Arctic science included a competition to give the laboratory a local name. The winning entry recognized the building's resemblance to a *Snowy Owl,* 1988. Photo: Michael Bravo

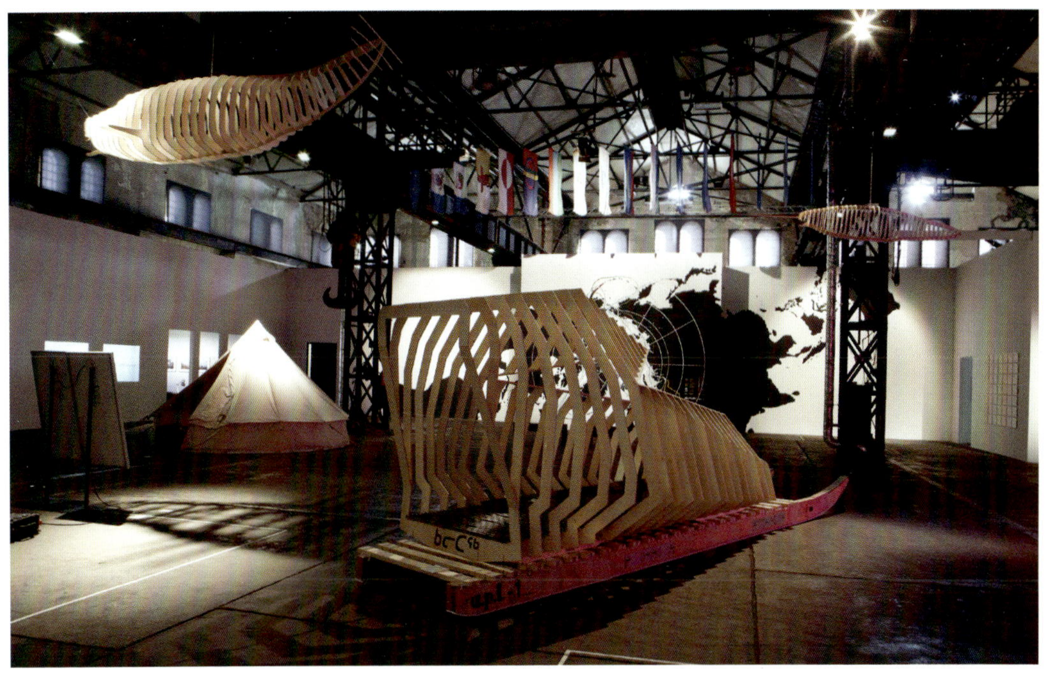

Plate 9
Arctic Perspective exhibition, HMKV at PHOENIX Halle Dortmund, June 18 – October 10, 2010.
Curated by Inke Arns, Matthew Biederman, Marko Peljhan. Photo: Nejc Trošt

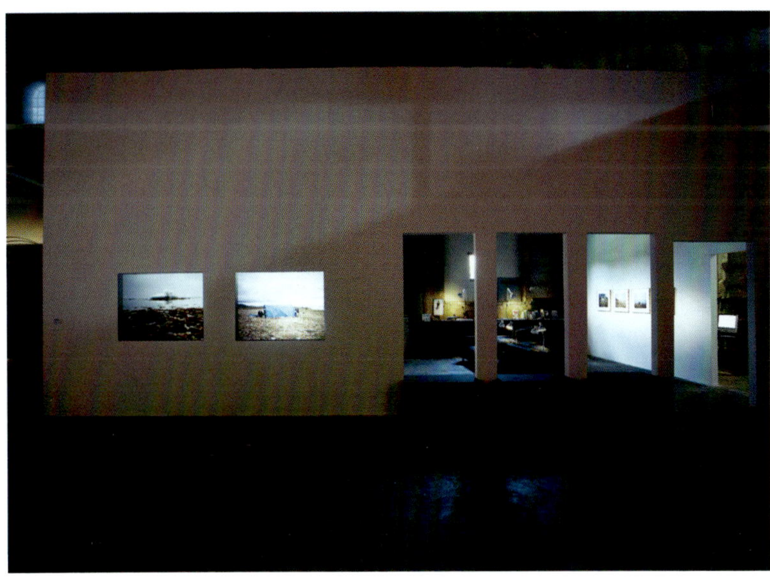

Plate 10
Arctic Perspective exhibition, HMKV at PHOENIX Halle Dortmund,
June 18 – October 10, 2010. Curated by Inke Arns, Matthew Biederman, Marko
Peljhan. Photo: Thomas Wucherpfennig, www.laborb.de

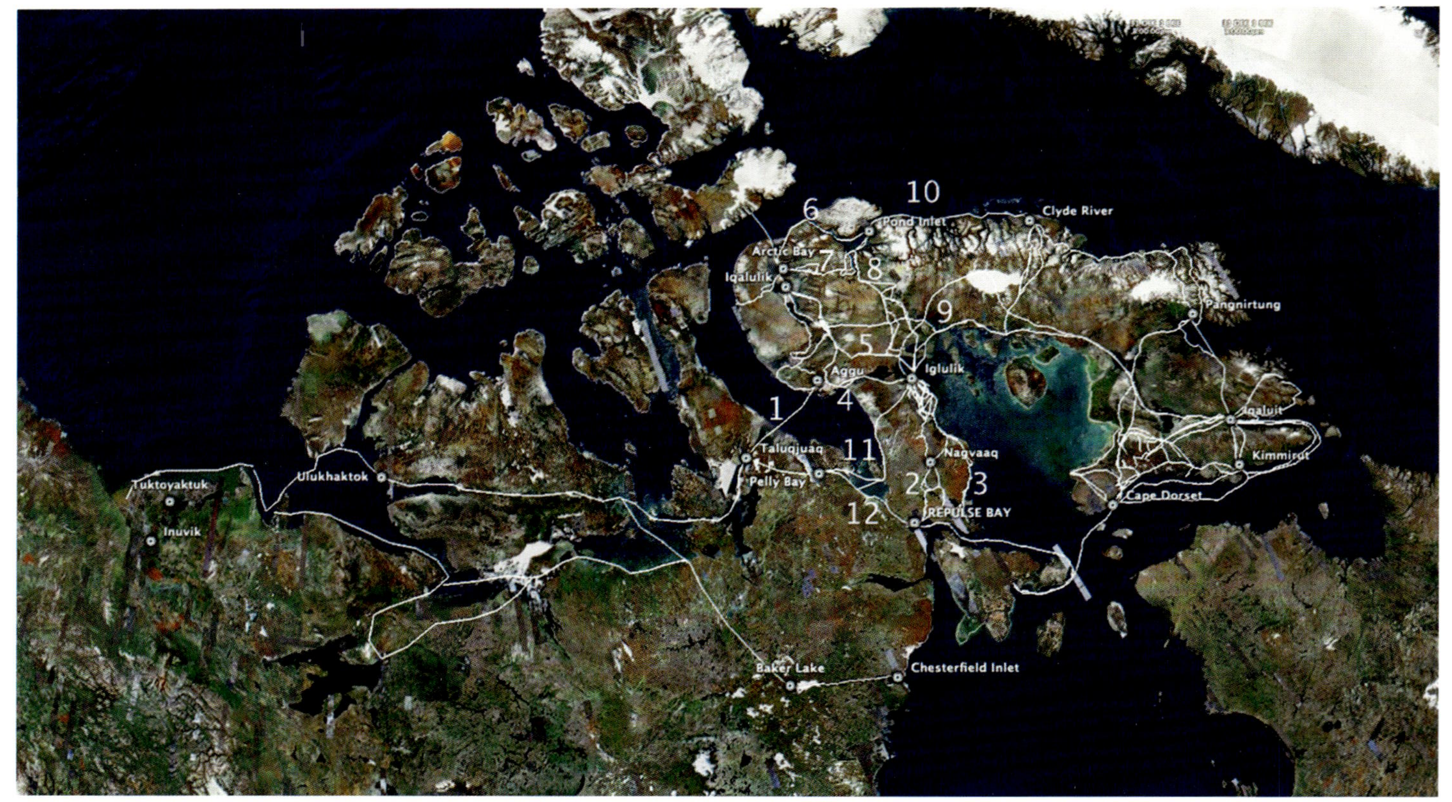

Plate 11
Map showing some sections of the network of Inuit Arctic trails covering Arctic Canada.
Image: Claudio Aporta, 2008. Reproduced from Claudio Aporta, "The Trail as Home:
Inuit and Their Pan-Arctic Network of Routes," *Human Ecology* 37, no. 2 (2009), pp. 131–46.

Arctic Perspective Cahier No. 2

Arctic Geopolitics & Autonomy

Edited by
Michael Bravo &
Nicola Triscott

Series editors
Inke Arns
Matthew Biederman
Marko Peljhan
Nicola Triscott

With the support of the Culture Programme
of the European Union

Culture Programme

This project has been funded with support from the
European Commission. This publication reflects the
views only of the authors, and the Commission cannot
be held responsible for any use which may be made of
the information contained therein.

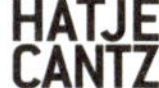

Credits

The Arctic Perspective Initiative is a collaboration with individuals and organizations in the North, and we would particularly like to thank

Paul Apak
Rhoda Arnakallak
Cheryl Ashton
Navarana Beveridge
Richard Carbonnier
Shari Gearheard
Taylor Inuaraq
Celina and Sandy Irngaut
Charlie Ittukssarjuat
Harry Ikerapik Ittuksarjuat
Thomas Anguti Johnson
Becky Kilabuk
Ralph Kownak
Zacharias Kunuk
John MacDonald,
Cornelius Nutarak Sr.
Philippa Ootoowak (Rebecca P Idlout Library)
Herve Paniaq
David "DJ" Panipak
Paul Quassa
George Qulaut
Guillaume Ittuksarjuat Salladin
Oana Spinu

ARTCIRQ
Igliniit project
Igloolik Isuma Productions
Inuit Heritage Trust
Kinngait Studios
Makivik Corporation
Mittimatilik Hunters & Trappers Organization
Nasivvik High School
Nattinak Visitor Center
Qikiqtani Inuit Association
Taqramiut Productions

The communities of Igloolik, Mittimatilik,
Hall Beach, and Iqaluit

Contents

14

Introduction

On the European Community agenda, Arctic geopolitics are "in," while sealskins are officially "out." Hardly a day passes without yet another news story about a race for resources in the Arctic. The states with waterfronts on the Arctic Ocean—Canada, Denmark, Norway, Russia, and the United States—have been largely cooperating to settle their low-level boundary issues and to meet United Nations deadlines for submitting surveys of their continental shelves. The prospect of exploiting new oil and natural gas energy reserves for G8 markets is redefining the Arctic as a strategic environment. The promise of a practical northern sea route over Russia brought about by diminishing sea ice is turning the attention of powerful Asian shipping states northward. Our contributing specialist on geopolitics to this volume, Lassi Heininen, thinks that the Arctic is experiencing a profound set of political, economic, and environmental changes, which other experts agree constitute a "state change" in the Arctic itself.[1]

In the face of global environmental concern, there is a grave danger that the autonomy of ordinary people who actually live in the Arctic is being sidelined by much more powerful strategic interests. The inhabited Arctic is no less international in its politics and economics than the rest of the world. There is, however, an enormous gulf separating the experience and understanding of those who live in the Arctic and those who do not but are employed to advise or lobby for regulating it.

In late 2009 I was approached by the organizers of the Arctic Perspective Initiative, a transnational art, science, and culture collaboration, to edit a collection of essays to situate their project in its geopolitical context. Collaborating periodically with artists has previously been important in the development of my own work. My debts to Inuit artists go back to 1988 when, having finished my training as a satellite communications engineer, I met Zacharias Kunuk in Igloolik, a small Inuit community in Nunavut that is now the principal site of this project. Kunuk, an internationally acclaimed video-maker, has throughout his artistic career resisted political affiliation, a position grounded in his anticolonial politics. My working collaboration with Kunuk has, for my part, been a source of intellectual freedom rooted in dialogue about landscape, history, and decolonization. The central premise in this book, that competing spatial narratives about the Arctic can be embodied and performed by using technologies to create autonomy, owes a significant debt to my conversations with Kunuk about telecommunications and storytelling. Readers will recognize that the spatial narratives privileged in this book are not necessarily those that sit easily alongside traditional geopolitical writing.

While universities can encourage independent political critique, just as many researchers appear comfortable to be aligned with or sponsored by geopolitical interests. Intellectual freedom asks that we are reflexive and transparent in applying our critiques to our own politics. Recognizing the political conditions of one's own freedoms is the precondition

[1]

Alun Anderson, *After the Ice: Life, Death, and Geopolitics in the New Arctic* (New York, 2009); Oran Young, "Whither the Arctic? Conflict or Cooperation in the Circumpolar North, *Polar Record* 45, no. 1 (2008), pp. 73–82

for building political autonomy capable of resisting exploitation and repression. With that spirit of reflection in mind, this book is a work-in-progress reflecting a set of ongoing conversations between a small number of artists, indigenous peoples, scholars, and journalists.

Collaboration with the arts has a critical role to play in Arctic geopolitics. Thinking geographically first and foremost is an act of spatial and visual imagination. The public imagination of the Arctic is guided and framed by map projections, satellite imagery, photographs, and other forms of visual representation. Visual languages contain arguments, conceal interests, and highlight positions and perspectives. The role that different visual grammars and syntaxes play in shaping debates about the Arctic deserves more critical enquiry.

The Arctic Perspective Initiative (API) comprises an international group of individuals and non-profit organizations, including HMKV (Germany), Projekt Atol (Slovenia), C-TASC (Canada), Lorna (Iceland), and the Arts Catalyst (UK). It aims to move beyond the dominant visual discourses in the geopolitics of the Arctic through a series of interventions in media and communications technologies in collaboration with people in the community of Igloolik, and other small settlements, in Canada's High Arctic.

Igloolik hosts a permanent population of only 1,500 people, but it has for centuries been a crossroads and meeting place for Inuit peoples or *miut*. Comparable to a caravanserai on the Silk Road, Igloolik was a node along a network of trails, traditionally known for regrouping, resting, eating, socializing. The confluence

of trails around Igloolik span the width of the Canadian Arctic, and perhaps further to Alaska and Greenland.[2]

The "media-centric" approach of the API lead artists Marko Peljhan and Matthew Biederman is a collaborative, artistic, and technological response to Igloolik's own considerable arts and media history. Peljhan has come to Igloolik with a history of having explored how autonomy can be performed through technological experiments that have traveled to different kinds of extreme environments, initially setting out from his own country, Slovenia, around the time of its independence, which was replete with its own complexities of ethnicity and belonging.

In the volume's opening and closing essays, Nicola Triscott and Lassi Heininen identify a paradox of representation in the Arctic. The "political character" of technology, Triscott reminds us (cf. Langdon Winner), means that industrial technologies have shaped how large parts of the Arctic are governed, lived, and imagined. Yet in surveying the media, popular culture, and the arts in relation to the Arctic, Triscott observes that representations are overwhelmingly fixated with striking images of ice and polar bears, to the exclusion of any political complexities. Heininen observes that with few exceptions the dominant discourses of Arctic geopolitics are blind to the reality of the Arctic as an inhabited region in which communities have forged their livelihoods out of flexible and intimate relationships with their ecosystems; yet both peoples and ecosystems are repeatedly trivialized in both geopolitics and the arts.

Counteracting historical amnesia and contemporary self-interest and indifference goes to the heart of these essays. Together with the Arctic Perspective Initiative, they aim to ground perspectives on politics and art in technological interventions (that include broadband communications, environmental monitoring, satellite observation, video documentary

---

[2]
Mapping and interpreting the historical network of Inuit trails across the High Arctic lands, coasts, and seas of North America is part of an ongoing collaborative project—The Inuit Northwest Passage Laboratory, directed by Claudio Aporta and Michael Bravo.

—and writing) by making them embodied, geographically anchored to a specific strategic indigenous place, and politically self-aware.

My own essay shows how a history of interventions around technology have been critical in shaping ideas about Inuit autonomy and skill. Displays and performances of hunting equipment and techniques have cemented Igloolik's reputation as a site of a particular kind of traditional culture. Skills like kayaking that embody "autonomous masculinity" have fascinated ethnographic observers and served as a common currency for men to build relationships across cultural boundaries. However, this particular gendered rendering of autonomy is a two-edged sword. Nineteenth and twentieth century collectors and naturalists reckoned that hunting instruments were the measure of a society's rank, progress, and evolution. The classification systems of indigenous peoples into fixed cultural and spatial hierarchies, based on apparent technological sophistication, have had such a profound impact on popular and elite political imaginations as to construct lasting geopolitical barriers to indigenous political participation. In truth, Igloolik is a terrific place to find people rich in ideas and willing to experiment and innovate. What is, however, profoundly challenging for Inuit is to overcome the dysfunctional economic structure that has made northern Canada a provider of wealth and sovereignty for powerful elites in southern Canada, with a culture of dependence in return. As well as being a source of imagination and survival, technology then, when wrongly used, has created a deep structural legacy that has excluded indigenous peoples from full political and economic participation.

One significant question for the API to ask is what kind of spatial politics at the community level would produce a more just international order for the indigenous peoples of the Arctic. Recognizing the considerable political achievements of the Permanent Participants (indigenous organizations) in the Arctic Council as well as national organizations like the Inuit Tapiriit Kanatami, what kind of roles can communities play? Specifically, are there community-specific ways of experimenting with technology that suggest alternative political spatial orders? The strength of indigenous technology and the arts—they are essentially inseparable—across much of the Arctic should be a source of real optimism.

It's interesting then, as Katarina Soukup explains, to think about the Internet and digital broadcasting in terms that can be described as indigenous geopolitics. Eva Aariak, now the Premier of Nunavut, coined the term *ikiaqqivik* for "Internet" in the Inuktitut language, meaning "traveling through layers." Inuit have traditionally conceived of their cosmology in very spatial terms, drawing concentric circles around the earth up to the heavens. The advent of broadband communications can enable northern people to compress time and space (as shamans in the past had done) and to live at the speed dictated by international markets and exchanges. More importantly, the much richer multimedia capacities enabled by broadband open up the discursive space for communicating indigenous perspectives through technological performances and representations that are much more sympathetic to their cultural values. Because these technologies are not so narrowly textual, Soukup explains, they provide a means to articulate complex expressions of historical and political thinking that were previously denied by the cultural conservatism, or perhaps ethnocentrism, of histories wedded to the written word.

Here projects like the API can contribute to community-based spatial politics and priorities that are surprisingly close to home. Zacharias Kunuk grew up at his family outpost camp, Siuraarjuk, on the other side of the Ikiq, about fifteen miles across the sea from Igloolik. The power of the API "media-centric" approach was beautifully demonstrated through a live real-time conversation about contemporary nomadism between Kunuk and Biederman at Siuraarjuk, and a panel of artists, authors, and curators at a public API event hosted by the Canadian High Commission in London, in May 2010. Kunuk and the panelists discussed the significance of access to new technologies for the next generation of Inuit. The successful satellite-linked conversation raised an obvious question: why is high-bandwidth digital telecommunications access not *always* available throughout northern Canada rather than just in the centers of habitation? These other spaces of tundra, coast, and sea are the Inuit Arctic, and in the new logic of the cross-platform digital world not being digitally connected increasingly implies economic marginalization. No wonder Kunuk's top priority is to have a full media center capability at his traditional camp. The contributors agree: new media technologies are essential for maintaining the vitality of narratives that give places meaning.

Since narratives lie so close to the heart of northern indigenous societies, it is tempting to ask how far they really can reach into the geopolitical domains of state-dominated power. David Turnbull invites us to pose the question differently and with profound implications. It's not that technologies carry narratives to new and difficult places. Narratives, he explains, are themselves technologies by which societies have for millennia navigated. The special quality of narratives, he argues, is that they are uniquely suited for traveling because they are able to hold complex combinations of knowledge in tension—and therefore together.

In keeping with the spirit of API, Turnbull's account is itself a story about the stories we tell of human movement out of Africa and around the world. Highlighting the role of movement in the ways we have come to know the world, he argues, destabilizes the dominant narrative of the journey out of Africa culminating in the sedentary civilization of Western Europe. Instead, he brings to the fore the last two great feats of human exploration—the Polynesian occupation of the Pacific and the Eskimo occupation of the Arctic. His essay contends that not only were the Eskimos and the Polynesians making real voyages of discovery, moving into literally unknown and unoccupied regions, they also developed socio-technical complexes enabling them to move in extremely difficult environments that are still central to their cultural identities today.

Technology complexes are social, cognitive, material, and narratological; these are the basis of the complex adaptive systems that have enabled nomadic peoples to live strategically and flexibly. The absence of these qualities and the considerable reliance of the world's major economies on systems of standardized, mono-crop agrarian societies is conversely reflected in a loss of flexibility and responsiveness that endangers our capacity to survive unprecedented change. Finally, we return to Lassi Heininen's explicitly geopolitical reflections as he calls for an environmental "awakening" as the Arctic becomes more tightly coupled than ever with the rest of the globe. Can we learn from the kinds of media experiments in narrative taking place in Igloolik and elsewhere? Can international discussions about the Arctic environment move beyond political lobbying and jockeying for position of familiar vested interests? Our narratives and collective self-understanding enabled us to prosper in Polynesia and the Arctic. Do we have the narrative technologies for equitable sharing that will enable us to navigate through uncharted waters in the coming decades and perhaps centuries?

Michael Bravo
with Nicola Triscott

Critical Art and Intervention in the Technologies of the Arctic

Nicola Triscott

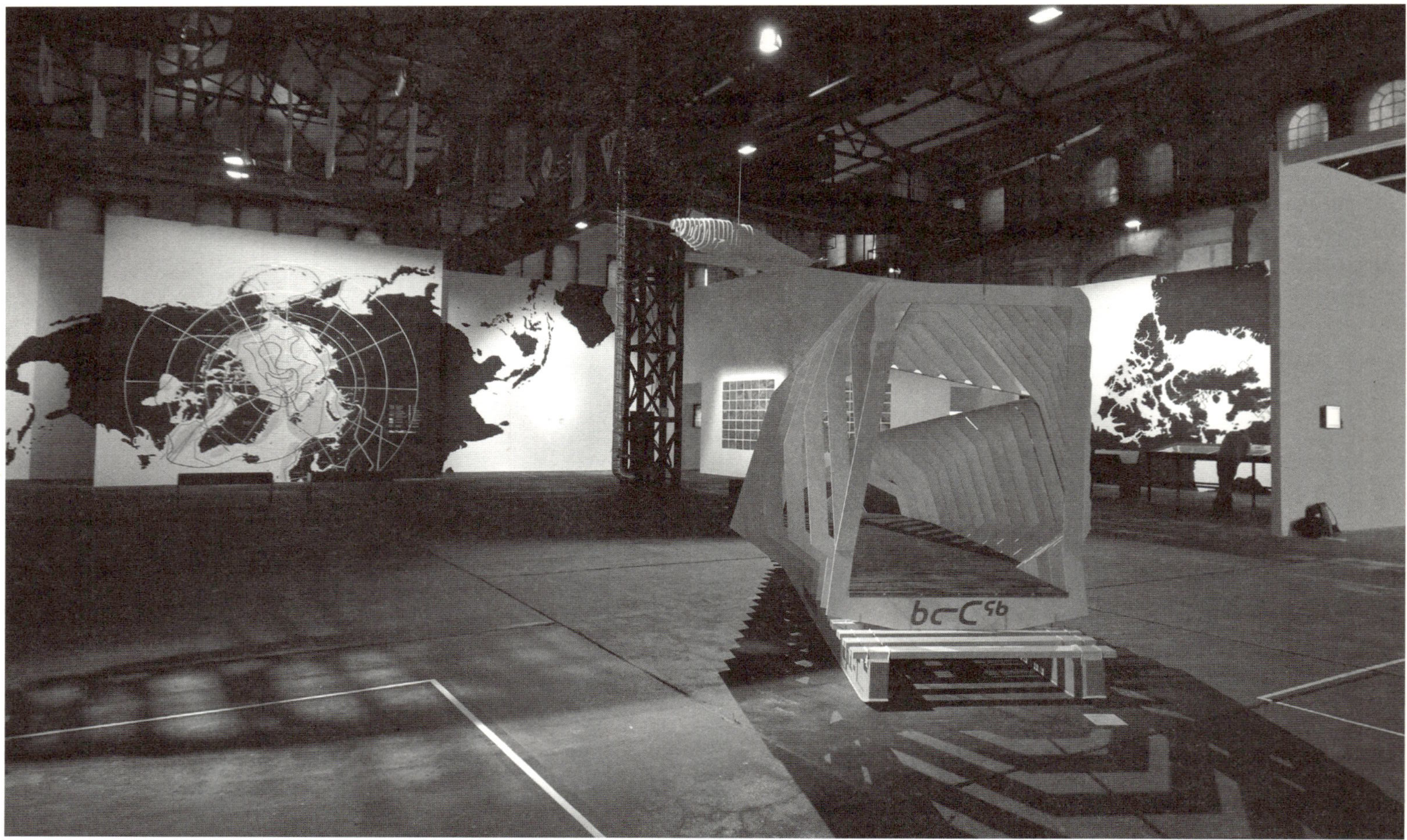

Arctic Perspective exhibition, HMKV at PHOENIX Halle Dortmund, June 18 – October 10, 2010. Curated by Inke Arns, Matthew Biederman, Marko Peljhan. Photo: Thomas Wucherpfennig, www.laborb.de

Heading north toward the pole, disparate worlds collide. High-tech electronic fortresses and entrenchments are sited here, and submarines glide beneath the ice. Oil extraction plants, mines, launch sites, and nuclear reactors dot the fringes of the Arctic landmasses, interspersed with scientific research stations and remote settlements. On this harsh, sparsely populated landscape, people still live, travel, and hunt across the softening tundra and sea ice. Livelihoods have profoundly changed since these technological structures came to the North, and now the impact of global warming threatens further change.

In the *Arctic Perspective* exhibition (ill. p.20) at the PHOENIX Halle in Dortmund,[1] the visitor enters through a darkened gallery, divided into two anechoic chambers. In each chamber, to either side of the viewer, lurk model submarines—one side, Russian, the other, American. The soundtrack in these rooms is of Inuit throat singing *(kattajaq),* a duet in which two women engage in a vocal contest to see who can outlast the other. The Arctic was the front line for the cold war, and it is still, it has been argued, an arena of tension. Interest in the high latitudes of the North has sharpened in recent times because of climate change and the need for energy and mineral resources.

Where the development, use, and trajectory of technology leads society is a critical issue anywhere in the world, but it has a particular urgency in the Arctic, where military, commercial, and political stakes are high. These stakes are amplified by the technological demands linked to the extreme climate. In this essay, I look at the cultural and political character of technology in the Arctic, through the lens of investigations and representations in the work of contemporary artists, to explore how they and nonaligned citizens, more broadly, are intervening in the politics of technology. I want to consider the significance of these interventions in relation to ideas of nomadism and autonomy in contemporary culture and the specific milieu of indigenous Arctic people's lives.

The "political character" of technology—as it has been termed by Langdon Winner—in the Arctic has tended to be shaped by forces controlled by strategic interests and commercial exploitation, rather than by the needs of the peoples of the Arctic or by the challenges presented by climate change.

In the Canadian High Arctic, Inuit societies—the small societies or *miut* groups of clusters of extended families within the Inuit world—for many centuries followed traditional patterns of a subsistence-led life that moved between well-known camps according to the seasons and the movements of the animal populations they were reliant on. Inuit long ago developed sophisticated technologies for surviving an environment that provided food, clothing, and shelter to satisfy all their needs, and

1
The *Arctic Perspective* exhibition documents the work of the Arctic Perspective Initiative (API). PHOENIX Halle, Dortmund, June 18 to October 10, 2010. Organized by HMKV and the API partners.

yet was also tinged by uncertainty and dangers that required respect and constant observation. By the early twentieth century, whalers and missionaries had traveled north into the High Arctic from Labrador and west from Greenland, bringing with them new materials and technologies—ships, guns, medicines, and luxury goods—as well as new laws, Bibles, and diseases. All of these were to exert a deep and lasting impact on Inuit. They showed themselves to be accomplished at adopting new technologies for their own needs and taking advantage of new economic opportunities.

The strategic importance of the Arctic for Canada's sovereignty grew in the decades following the First World War. The Arctic landscape for Inuit was traditionally a highly complex but well known network of trails across land, sea, and ice. It had been regarded by maritime powers as a maze of islands and channels, open at one moment and inaccessible at the next. The arrival of modern aircraft, however, heralded the promise of a new era of visibility and access from the air. Governments built airbases and radar stations in the Arctic to monitor the military movements of rival states, and new permanent settlements were developed around them. In the nineteen-sixties the government of Canada decided that all Inuit children should attend schools (and these schools emphasized different cultural traditions) and be enrolled in the principal institutions of the welfare state. Through incentives most Inuit were forced to vacate their traditional camps in order to meet the obligations that increasingly were attached to the settlements: wage labor, healthcare, and schools.

Across the Arctic Circle, Russia—and formerly, the Soviet Union—has long been northward looking and has regarded Siberia and the Russian Arctic as strategically important to the security of its heartland. Before World War II, the Soviet Union established many meteorological and radio stations in the Arctic. The Soviet Union placed military-industrial assets in the North, and this is the main reason why the Russian Arctic is so populated compared with the Canadian North. The ice-free waters surrounding the port of Murmansk gave it unique importance as the home of the Soviet Northern Fleet.

Energy and mineral resources have been key to the intense interest of Arctic-adjoining states in the High North. In the nineteen-sixties, the Canadian Arctic became the focus of an intensive search for oil, natural gas, and minerals. Oil fields were discovered in Alaska and on Canada's Ellesmere Island, accelerating efforts to explore further. Around the same period, huge reserves were also discovered in western Siberia. The Soviet Union constructed pipelines and created industrial centers for oil exploration and extraction, the beginning of economic dependence on exports from the region. The impact of the oil industry had a great impact on indigenous peoples across the

Circumpolar Arctic: in Canada, Scandinavia, Russia, and Siberia. In Siberia, the Khanty, traditional hunters and reindeer herders and once the ethnic majority in the region, are now a small minority among the settlers and migrant workers in the oil rich republic. Their once clean wilderness has been polluted by oil and damaged through deforestation, undermining the resilience of their traditional ways of life.

Another significant area of technological development in the Arctic is maritime transportation, driven by both commercial and strategic imperatives. The USA, Canada, and Russia have all been active in employing coastguard icebreakers, government research vessels, or military submarines to patrol the region. Commercial ships in the Arctic range from small fishing vessels to large cruise ships to gigantic container ships. The major shipping lanes currently run along the Norwegian coast into the Barents Sea and around the Kola Peninsula of northwest Russia. As global warming reduces the extent of multiyear Arctic sea ice, new shipping routes over northern Russia are opening up, while some local and north-south routes in northern Canada are becoming more navigable.

The Arctic is also a significant platform for science. During the International Geophysical Year (1957–58), more than 300 Arctic stations were established by northern countries. A major focus of scientific attention now, of course, is the effect of global warming on the cryosphere, and the impact of retreating glaciers, collapsing ice shelves, and shrinking concentrations of sea ice on the interlocking terrestrial, atmospheric, and ocean climate systems.

Despite this complex and inhabited technological landscape, representations of the Arctic in the media, popular culture, and the arts have tended to draw a rather different picture. Striking images of collapsing glaciers and polar bears adrift on icebergs in the media have shaped many people's perceptions of the Arctic as a remote, challenging, beautiful, and fragile expanse of ice sheet. This Arctic of the imagination occupies an important place in the thinking of many who will never go there, but it is also perpetuated by many who have. Rarely, despite the increasing interest in the Arctic, does the political complexity of the region find visual representation as a contested arena of aspirations—a fragile set of ecosystems that are simultaneously a storehouse of resources, both renewable and nonrenewable, a transport zone and a theater for military operations, as well as homelands to dozens of different indigenous groups.

I can think of many artworks by artists who have visited the North in recent years that reinforce the perception of a uniform landscape dominated by ice, stark beauty, and emptiness. I include some of those who have visited the Arctic with a specific and well-meaning "climate change" brief. However, in recent years there has been a growing number of artists' works that recognize a more complex situation in which the Arctic is understood as a territory with a history of large-scale scientific and technological experimentation and industrial exploitation. Oil exploration, mining, nuclear testing, cold war surveillance stations, advanced research installations, scientific and meteorological stations, and military bases in the Arctic region have all been the focus of attention, as have the impacts of these technologies on the Arctic's ecosystems. These are forming a group of works that counterbalance the body of representations depicting the Arctic as a parade of melting icebergs.

Nathalie Grenzhaeuser's photographic series *The Construction of the Quiet Earth,* 2007, (plates 3 & 4 p. 6, ills. p. 25) confronts us with the industrial transformation of the Arctic landscape. The photographs were taken in the Arctic archipelago of Svalbard. They show infrastructure from its mining history and modern scientific and research facilities. Grenzhaeuser's photographs are neither simple nor passive documentaries. Single moments and parts of the landscape are digitally recombined and over-layered. While giving an impression of beauty, with striking skies and wind-blown landscapes, the contrast of man-made industrial plants and high technology with cold, seemingly inhospitable landscapes is unsettling. Man is here, but not in human form, his presence detected from stark structures, metal buildings perched precariously on icy slopes, containers strewn across a plain, large pieces of machinery, bleak impersonal huts, high-tech satellite dishes, and strange domes scanning the skies.

The theme of industrial exploitation of the land is taken up in the Center for Land Use Interpretation's (CLUI) exhibition *The Trans-Alaska Pipeline* (ill. top p. 26). CLUI is a nonprofit research and education organization studying the nature and extent of human interaction with the landscape in North America. Without being explicitly critical, CLUI artists produce detailed photographic evidence and other forms of documentation of contested sites—nuclear test sites, military installations, oil fields. CLUI's *Trans-Alaska Pipeline* exhibition was an extensive series of photographs and maps examining in detail the four-foot wide, 800 mile-long pipe, which spans the entire state from top to bottom, bringing the entirety of oil extracted from Prudhoe Bay in the Arctic Circle—the largest oil field in the United States—to market. The pipeline, the exhibit explains, "created overland access across the Last Frontier . . . and brought billions of dollars to natives, Alaskan residents, construction workers, and, of course, the oil companies."

Several artists have looked at the legacy and contemporary existence of military technologies in the Arctic. Charles Stankievech's *The DEW Project*, 2009 (ill. bottom p. 26), for example, is a multimedia work inspired by the joint US-Canadian military

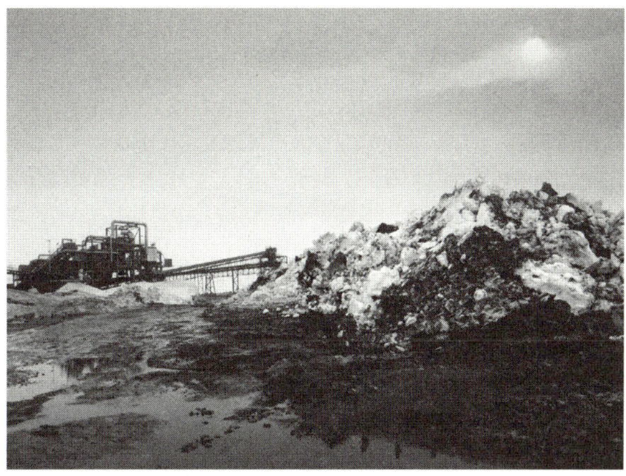

Nathalie Grenzhaeuser, *Schmelze,* 2007, from the series
The Construction of the Quiet Earth. LightJet print, Diasec
matte, 120 x 160 cm, edition 5 & 2 AP

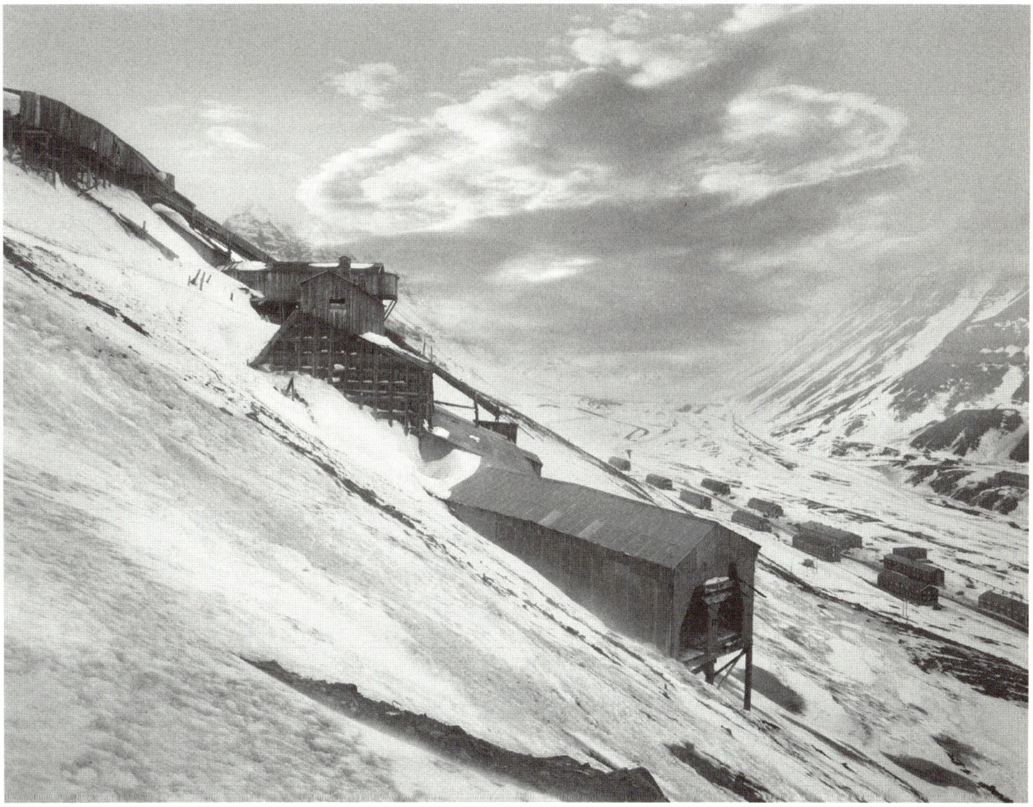

Nathalie Grenzhaeuser, *Zuckerhut,* 2007, from the series
The Construction of the Quiet Earth. LightJet print, Diasec matte, 120 x 160 cm, edition 5 & 2 AP

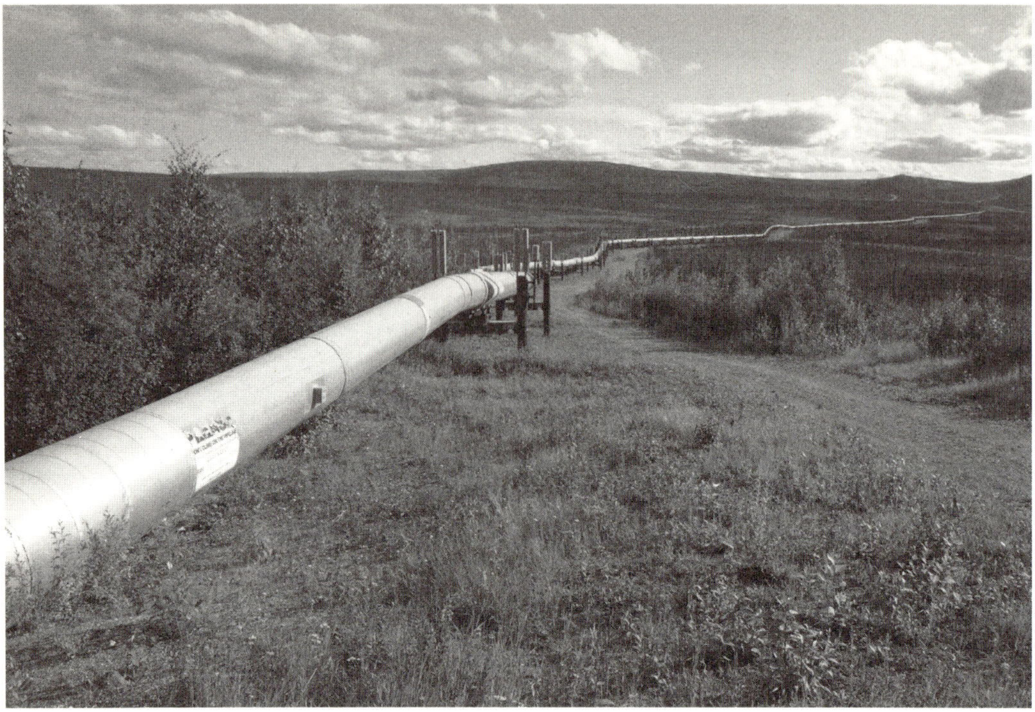

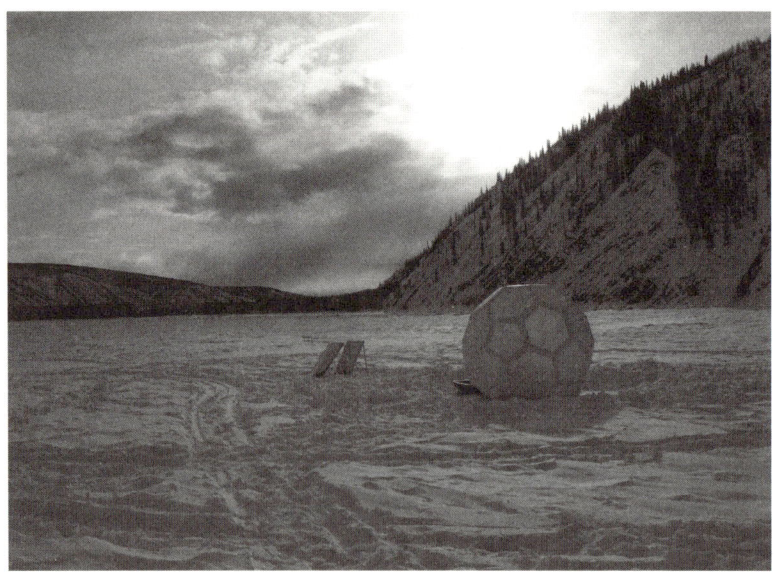

Center for Land Use Interpretation, *The Trans-Alaska Pipeline.*

Charles Stankievech, *The DEW Project,* field Installation at the
Yukon and Klondike River confluence, 2008.

radar network, Distant Early Warning Line. This was a system of radar stations in the far northern Arctic region of Canada, with additional stations along the north coast and islands of Alaska, the Faroe Islands, Greenland, and Iceland. The DEW Line was set up to detect incoming Soviet bombers during the cold war. The field installation component of Stankievech's project featured a geodesic dome on the frozen confluence of the Yukon and Klondike Rivers, a remote sculptural installation which also acted as a distant listening station, allowing people to listen to the river flow and ice shifting via submerged hydrophones, and broadcasting those sounds via radio station and the Internet.

Another of CLUI's projects documents Thule airbase in Greenland. This isolated American outpost is the largest, northernmost community on the planet, home to 1,100 people, all of whom live and work at the base. Built in 1951 as a refueling station for American bombers, Thule airbase caused the forced relocation of Inuit to the neighboring location of Qanaaq. Thule exists today to support two radar and telemetry stations and a long runway capable of servicing large military aircraft. CLUI's aim is to make a documentation project, with little critical interpretation, leaving the viewers to form their own interpretations and opinions.

In those spaces beyond our familiar world, such as those of advanced technology, the polar regions, oceans, and deep space—where cultural imaginaries have long competed with more factual reports—we are perhaps as apt to believe the storytellers as the scientists or spokesmen. In 2009, the Palais de Tokyo in Paris organized the exhibition *Gakona*, featuring artworks by Micol Assaël, Ceal Floyer, Laurent Grasso, and Roman Signer, which played with facts, rumor, science, and imagination surrounding modern technology. Gakona is a village in Alaska, home to the American HAARP research program (High-frequency Active Auroral Research Program), which studies the transmission of electricity in the uppermost portion of the atmosphere. HAARP is surrounded by a cloud of rumor and conspiracy theory; its forest of antennas have been blamed for disrupting climate, beaming hazardous electromagnetic waves, influencing human behavior, and feared as an advanced weaponry, able to disrupt weather and communications over large parts of the planet. Laurent Grasso's work *HAARP* for the Gakona exhibition looked very like the field of antennas at the Gakona facility, a large construction of metal poles and wires, connected to black boxes on the floor. Visitors were not allowed to enter the room, although the antennas were apparently not connected to receivers. Was this to elicit a frisson of paranoia, simply to avoid damage, or to echo the discourse of security that surrounds many modern technological installations?

In contrast, Bureau d'Études, a French art collective specializing in mapmaking, produced a map that purports to offer a factual and objective display of military and industrial activity in the Arctic, *Conquête du Grand Nord*, for the @rt Outsiders festival in 2009. The map shows military bases, nuclear reactors, radar stations, posts, sites of nuclear tests, mines, oil extraction plants, and polluted areas.

Two films by the Russian artist Pavel Medvedev have explored the impact of technology and industrialization on people living in the Russian Arctic. Medvedev makes short yet complex and intensely visual documentary portraits of some of post-Soviet Russia's most isolated people and places. In his 2002 film *Vacation in November*, landscapes of white snowfields in northern Russia contrast with scenes in the blackness of the region's mines, seen through the headlamps of the miners. But this initial visual contrast between the traditional snowscapes populated by reindeer herders and the gritty dirt of the mining industry is gradually peeled away in Medvedev's film, uncovering a more complex, interlinked reality. The reindeer herders, it turns out, are in fact miners on vacation, and at the end of their round-up of the reindeers, they slaughter the creatures with clubs, skinning the carcasses for fur and meat. They must do this because the mine has cut their wages in the post-Soviet years, and they can no longer afford to live on their salaries alone.

Medvedev's 2006 film *On the Third Planet from the Sun* is a haunting picture of life in the country's Arctic Arkhangelsk region, where inhabitants forage in swamplands for scrap metal left behind from rocket launches in a region where H-bombs were tested. "I present ordinary people in problematic situations," Medvedev says, "but I don't try to elicit pity. I see these people as fully developed, living their lives as they find them. My task is to respect them and show how they are interesting. I dream that the lives of my characters might be better, but my only job is to film them. The more films like these are shown, the more public opinion would pressure for change."

Langdon Winner (1986) developed an analysis of the political character of technology, arguing that the physical arrangements of industrial production, warfare, communications, etc., have not only transformed the exercise of power and the experience of citizenship, but they have also introduced "inherently political technologies" which are, by their very nature, centralized or decentralized, egalitarian or inegalitarian, repressive or liberating.

Following this analysis, one way to look at emerging technologies is to consider the extent to which they lock people into certain systems or, conversely, enable users to adapt them to fit their own purposes, resources, knowledge, and culture. There are highly centralized and controlled technologies, such as centralized nuclear power and genetically modified (GM) crops, that offer very little, if any, flexibility for how they are used, and require very specific infrastructures and systems to support them. At the other end of the spectrum, there are examples of participatory technologies that provide an open platform for new sorts of use, such as microrenewable energy, intermediate technologies for agriculture and the Linux operating system, technologies that place control for usage and further development in the hands of the user (Stilgoe, 2007).

A question, therefore, that could be asked of any emerging technology is whether it is locking us into one system or providing scope for openness and autonomous use. Another is whether the technology has been developed specifically to benefit people—the users—or to serve commercial or military interests. Most science and technology is not human-centered. It is developed for a range of economic, military, and social reasons, but rarely any that put the long-term good of people in general and the planet as the primary objective. The operational framework for scientific development primarily derives from the strategic and commercial importance attached to advanced technologies, including nuclear energy/weaponry and space technology. The spread of technology, particularly in the developed world, then comes through a partnership between science and industry. Often, new technologies are developed through military applications, for warfare, before gradually filtering into civilian industries, and then into civilian use. (Chapman, Yudkin, 1992) This can be seen in the cases of the personal computer, the Internet, imaging systems, and telecommunications.

These processes seem to be out of the control of the wider citizenry, whose everyday lives are nonetheless shaped by the systems, products, and discoveries resulting from scientific and technological research. The question then arises as to how people, encouraged to be passive in the face of powerful knowledge elites, can reassert some autonomy by shaping the content and direction of science and technology.

The strategies by which citizens have tried to affect, or disrupt, the centralized systems of science and technology, have been explored—and in some cases pioneered—by artists whose work intervenes socially and politically in the public realm. Tactics include involvement in early stage research and development (which Winner identifies as the critical point for shaping an emerging technology), the sharing of expertise and knowledge between specialists and non-specialists, illegal or unregulated use, civil disobedience, citizen appropriation of scientific and technological applications, independent or collaborative development, political action, and diplomacy.

The artist Ashok Sukumaran has produced a series of projects developing and exploring the concept of "leakage," the illegal or unregulated use of technology. He considers that an alternative history of many technologies could be written as a series of attempts, not to communicate information or transfer benefits, but rather "to insulate, or isolate, unwanted forces or state or commercial secrets from others." Often this notion of insulation has a practical dimension in the nature of the technology, such as in electrical insulation or in isolating nuclear waste, but it also includes the commercial imperative to control the products of technology, and to control knowledge and expertise. In all this, Sukumaran notes: "the phenomena of 'leakage,' such as the stealing of over 30% of electrical power in the Indian grid, or the constant stream of 'pirate' production of digital resources, exists as a continuous mirror. Power flows, leaks, out of the official system into various 'illegitimate' venues."[2]

These concerns invoke questions of property, ownership and of access rights. Sukumaran's work *sharing_01*, 2007 (ills. p. 31), part of his ongoing project on electricity in the urban environment, involved a ninth-floor resident of a block of apartments on the wealthy Carter Road in Mumbai who agreed to "share" two electrical connections in her house with a temporary occupant of the road below. A switchboard on a wall by the road gave control of the electrical connections in the house and, on the road, a 60 watt bulb and a standing fan were located. The light and the fan were made available to street food vendors. Passers by could also determine the "balance" between the two consumers. The two supplies were moderated to ensure that the total consumption did not exceed what the house would use normally. For instance, when the vendors took more electricity, the house received less and its lights dimmed.

Sukumaran's project is a useful source of reflection for the purpose of this cahier in that it demonstrates a technology (the electrical system) with an infrastructure so inflexible and controlled that even those with the necessary wealth (the vendor) cannot easily benefit from it. However, by a small artistic intervention and act of cooperation, the system is shared, for a while at least. In "real life," the vendor would either need to join those members of Indian society who illegally tap the electrical system or set up his own generator or—in the spirit of API—purchase a solar panel.

"Leakage" and interception activities extend across the spectrum of the informal economy, from the unregulated to the illegal. The history of the informal economy, as with the history of leakage, has been integral to continuing attempts on the part of governments and institutions to control and regulate aspects of their economies, which increasingly include technological developments. No such regulation has ever been wholly enforceable.

Since 1993, the American arts collective Critical Art Ensemble (CAE) has critiqued through its writings and artistic practice the processes and politics of biotechnology, one of the least publicly understood technologies of our time, and an area that is highly controlled and regulated. CAE's actions aim to involve

2
Ashok Sukumaran
(unpublished, untitled,
2008).

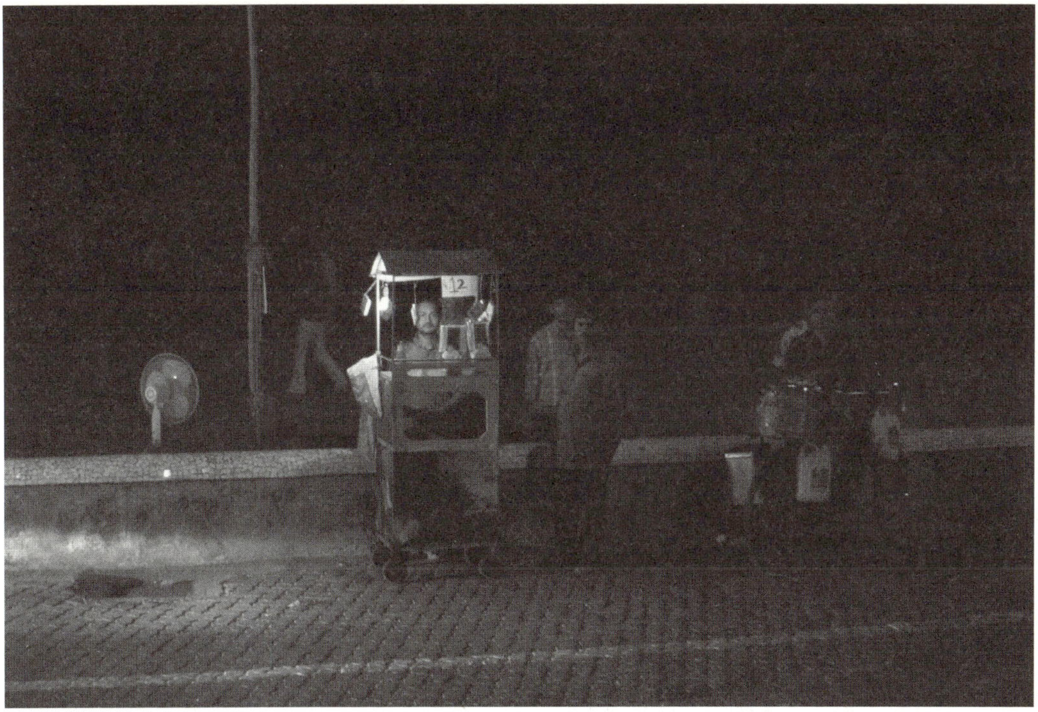

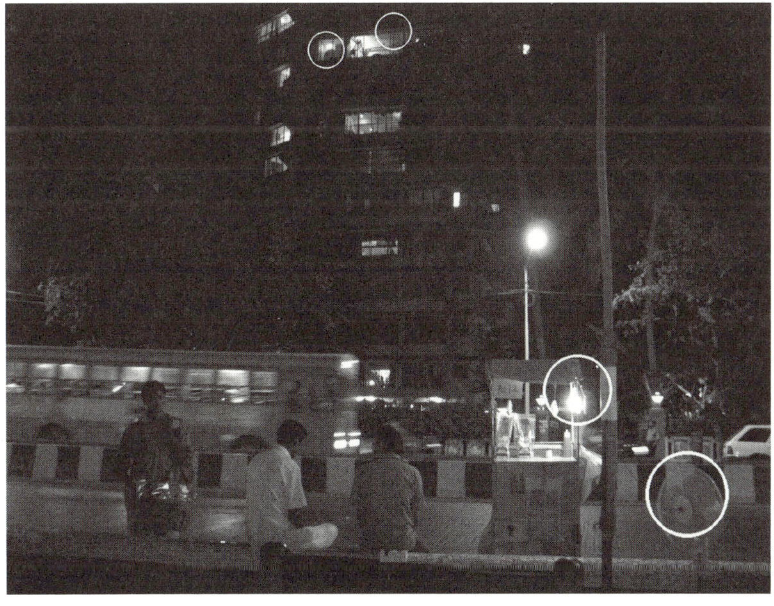

Ashok Sukumaran, *sharing_01*, street vendor. A dimmer switch on the promenade wall gives control of the two connections in the apartment, and (on the road) a 60 watt bulb and a standing fan.

Ashok Sukumaran, *sharing_01*, view of the apartment, vendor's cart, and the shared connections. The fan and light by the cart and in the apartment are circled.

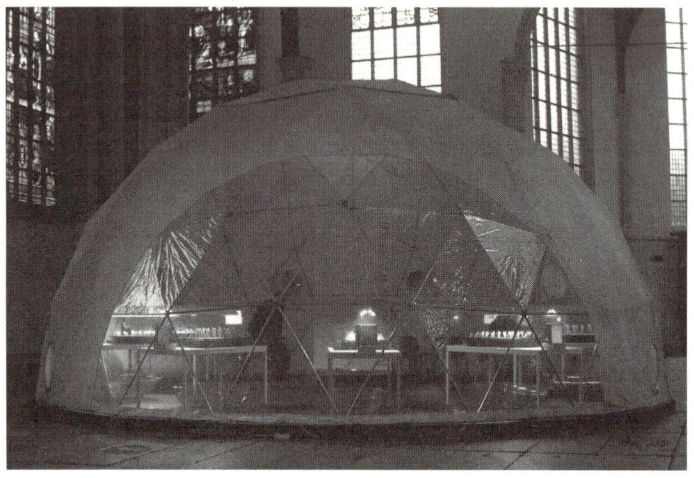

Critical Art Ensemble, Beatriz da Costa, Claire Pentecost,
Molecular Invasion, 2002

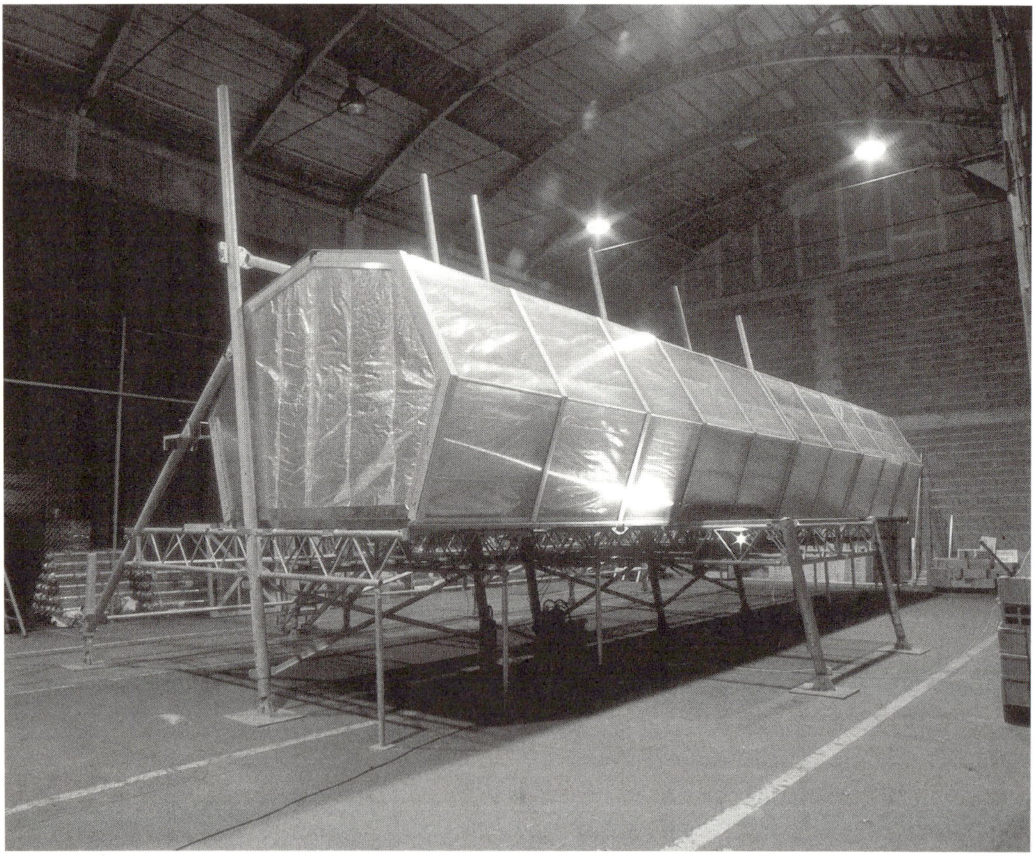

Makrolab mkII, overhaul, Projekt Atol / Marko Peljhan, Aljaž Lavrič,
Matevž Frančič, 1999, photo: Miha Fras

people in the routine processes of biotechnology, to let them see and use them, and realize that they can understand biotechnology if they wish and can participate in the discourse around it.

One key area in which CAE aims to stir debate is the appropriation of food production systems by major corporations, specifically by the promotion and distribution of genetically modified (GM) food systems. In their performance work *Free Range Grain,* 2003–4, CAE constructed a portable, public lab, inviting the public to bring food products labeled as "GM-free" or organic and to test them to see if this really was the case (often it was not). In *Molecular Invasion,* 2002–4 (ill. top p. 32), CAE developed this critique into a tactical response to corporate agricultural biotechnology and attempted to "reverse-engineer" genetically modified canola, corn, and soy plants through the use of nontoxic chemical disrupters. In an accompanying text, CAE presented their critique of corporate biotechnology and outlined a series of "contestational biology" tactics, taking ideas of civil disobedience into bioscience. Contestational biology must be conducted, according to CAE, by directly engaging biology (biotechnology) itself in order to disrupt the course of profit back to the biotech corporations such as Monsanto.

Notions of interception and leakage, and of direct engagement with technology, have been integral to some of the works of one of API's lead artists Marko Peljhan.[3] When Makrolab—Peljhan's nomadic research station developed and tested between 1997 and 2007 (ill. bottom p. 32)—was installed for the first time in 1997 at the exhibition Documenta X in Kassel, the lab residents using its broadcasting and receiving aerials, tapped into communications, routed via international Inmarsat tele-communication satellites, capturing private telephone conversations, satellite-controlled navigation systems, and military and economic communications.

Makrolab, as an idea, was born in 1994 on the island of Krk, off the Croatian coast, with the Yugoslav civil wars raging in the skies. Peljhan's initial purpose was to establish an independent, self-sufficient performance and research structure, an isolated outpost for survival and a critical reflection of the societal conditions in which he and his collaborators found themselves. The ultimate goal was to design a system that could work in a hostile environment, both for humans and for technology. Makrolab subsequently evolved in remote and isolated areas of Scotland, Australia, Slovenia, Italy, and Finland, with independent research projects undertaken by its changing crews in the broad zones of telecommunications, climate, and migration patterns.

In considering his response to the changing geopolitical and social circumstances in Eastern Europe and the world, and the unveiling of previously invisible divisions and political preferences, Peljhan became interested in the process of "conversion." This is the way in which military-industrial technologies gradually filter into the civilian domain. Peljhan set out to short-circuit this process and convert these technologies for tactical and artistic/media use.

Interested in radio and telecommunications, and researching military strategy, Peljhan has been particularly aware of surveillance technologies and the ability of intelligence specialists to monitor the communications infrastructure and to precisely locate, record, and analyze much of what was being done in the electromagnetic spectrum. He has noted, too, that telecommunication laws and the interests of telecommunications monopolies tend to suppress new and independent media. He has developed a critical and practical interest in setting up autonomous communications networks for artists and progressive social advocates. Radio is key to his research: he founded and coordinates the Insular Technologies initiative, which proposed an autonomous high frequency radio network long before the advent of wireless Internet. As long ago as 1997, he suggested building a global independent satellite telecommunications network, an alternative to the Intelsat system. His interests have extended logically into developing citizen surveillance and sensing strategies, and have found a new home and exigency in the High North of Canada's Arctic.

While the tactics of artists and those interested in social change have frequently focused on empowering people by giving them information about technologies and access to them, increasing access to knowledge and information does not automatically enhance democracy. Genuine democracy, as Winner understood, involves the pursuit of common ends through discussion, deliberation, and collective decision-making. An additional tactic suggested by Bruno Latour in his book *The Politics of Nature*: *How to Bring the Sciences into Democracy* is the ancient art of diplomacy. Latour explains that there will always be conflicting versions of reality among different groups of people and deliberates about how this situation can best be handled. He suggests that diplomacy—the management of communications and relationships between nations or groups, or, in its modern form, the skill of resolving differences through agreement and harmony, provides one workable method.

API works with this notion of diplomacy on two levels: first, in its methodology it adopts an inclusive and open working strategy with the people of the Arctic. Second, it introduces free and open media systems to help enable indigenous peoples of the North to communicate directly between themselves and with people in the South.

Traditional technologies of indigenous Arctic peoples were designed for a flexible, nomadic lifestyle. Their technologies were mobile, resilient to harsh conditions, adaptable to changing circumstances, and dependent on sharing skills, resources, and knowledge throughout the extended family and society. Within the span of just a few generations, Inuit communities have undergone a huge transition. New settled living and working arrangements, technologies, education, and commercial systems brought wholesale by external institutions have changed and threatened Inuit traditions, customs, skills, and languages.

Inuit and other indigenous Arctic people have adapted to these new circumstances and technological systems. Many Inuit have—as Michael Bravo notes—become accomplished technophiles, actively incorporating and adapting new technologies into their everyday lives. Rifles and snowmobiles are frequently cited examples, but the Inuit appropriation and development of broadcasting and filmmaking to sustain and promote their own culture and interests are also notable interventions in the politics of technology.[4] Likewise, Lassi Heininen has observed how indigenous groups have organized themselves using technologies associated with institutions of law and diplomacy to exert pressure on governments and corporations in support of their interests.

Despite these rapid changes to the fabric of their societies, Inuit have remained closely tied to the land. When the opportunity arises, some Inuit still leave their communities and live out on the land for a time. As Katarina Soukup's essay demonstrates, there is a very active interest in utilizing new technologies that can enhance and enable a "contemporary nomadism," the ability to move, work, and live on the land while remaining in contact with communities and having access to new media and environment-monitoring technologies.

In recent decades, the concept of "nomadism" has had a popular makeover in contemporary culture and cultural studies, in North American literature as well as in the European avant garde. Contemporary notions of nomadism include the perpetual traveler and the "technomad"—a nomadic cyber lifestyle. The use of the "nomadic" as a discourse—whether philosophical, literary, technological, or physical—involves a rejection of borders and boundaries, and a move to escape the confines of fixed identities of nationality, religion, economic status, or gender. In their book *A Thousand Plateaus*, Gilles Deleuze and Pierre-Félix Guattari refer frequently to the idea of philosophical nomadism: a line of enquiry and approach that requires an ability to think outside of the dominant structure. Those who move from one place to another, who do not "belong" in any one physical space, those who refuse to accept the conditions of the State, those who subvert—these embody Deleuze and Guattari's concept of "nomadology." More than a lifestyle choice, Deleuze and Guattari saw nomadology as an alternative approach to understanding the history of civilization, providing multiple narratives and suggesting an alternative

4
In the nineteen-seventies it was clear to Inuit leadership that television—able to fill every living room in the Arctic with images depicting southern attitudes, values, and behaviors—represented a new and potentially devastating threat to Inuit language and culture. The Inuit Broadcasting Corporation was set up as a response and, since 1981, has been making and broadcasting programs about Canadian Inuit culture for Inuit people in their own language of Inuktitut. In 1990, Igloolik Isuma Productions became Canada's first Inuit independent film and TV (and now Internet) production company.

References
Langdon Winner, *The Whale and the Reactor: A Search for Limits in an Age of High Technology* (Chicago, 1986).

Jack Stilgoe, *Nanodialogues: Experiments in Public Engagement with Science* (London, 2007).

Gary Chapman and Joel Yudken, *A Briefing Book on the Military-Industrial Complex* (Washington, D.C., 1992).

Bruno Latour, *Politics of Nature: How to Bring the Sciences into Democracy* (Cambridge MA, 2004).

Gilles Deleuze and Pierre-Felix Guattari, *A Thousand Plateaus*, trans. Brian Massumi (London, 2004).

history to that of territories, grand designs, and institutions in traditional historical narratives.

One should be very cautious in suggesting there is real common ground between "nomadism" as a term of the way of life of traditional indigenous hunting societies and the more recent concept of "nomadism," but it is perhaps unsurprising that traditional nomadic lifestyles hold an appeal for artists, with their sense of autonomy rooted in a shared history of mobility across borders, and social values that were hostile to the use of coercion and interference in the affairs of others.

In the Arctic Perspective Initiative, the concept of a nomadology of thought and the contemporary Inuit way of life, with its deep ties to the land and its flexibility and adaptability, come together. The goal of the API project is to design and develop a system of mobile technologies and infrastructure to support and enhance contemporary seminomadic or seasonally-nomadic livelihoods. This goal is underlain by utopian notions of autonomy, and an understanding of the social and political character of technology, with the knowledge that to set up sustainable systems needs a structural approach that starts from the interests, knowledge, and lifestyles of the people for whom it is designed.

Indigenous Arctic people have adapted to changing political and environmental circumstances. They have negotiated gigantic land settlements, set up cross-national political groups, secured high levels of self-determination in Nunavut and Greenland, lobbied for better land management, protected their own culture and language with self-run broadcasting and film companies, and become prominent in media coverage of climate change. By designing their own technological systems —using free and open technologies and utilizing sustainable energy—indigenous people of the North would be better placed to develop technological infrastructures that fit their own resources, knowledge, and cultures, and place control for their further development firmly in their own hands.

Building Autonomy through Experiments in Technology and Skill

Michael Bravo

Is it a truism that men, regardless of country and culture, love gadgets? The pleasure of using technological devices also seems to apply to Inuit men, at least most of those I know in Canada's northeastern Arctic territory of Nunavut. And if this is so, perhaps "gadgets and gear" are a common pastime, even a shared language, for certain kinds of blokeish men from everywhere and all walks of life. Does this offer any insights into how men build political and cultural *autonomy* for their societies, which goes beyond conspicuous consumption?

Taking apart and repairing 85 horsepower outboard engines, experimenting with new pocket-size GPS receivers, driving bigger and badder SUVs definitely speaks to a certain Inuit masculinity, reflected in the kinds of activities that count as "work": making, fixing, moving. This *autonomous masculinity* carries associations of independence, mobility, and a strong sense of the male individual self. Locating the source of autonomy in work is difficult to pin down. This is partly because autonomy is a theoretical concept with multiple philosophical meanings that evade simple definitions. For instance, does the autonomy in the work of a hunter reside in the skillful control and coordination of the human body? Or is it located in the work that the technological device itself is capable of performing, and then extended to the person using it? Or is this autonomy more like an ironic or reflexive gesture, an aesthetic self-awareness of one's relationship to landscapes where the conditions are constantly changing? Perhaps in this latter sense, autonomy speaks to a shared sense of self-regulation and not something that can be bought or consumed.[1]

Inuit culture has long been admired for a specific set of idealized hunting technologies. If you imagine peeling away the veneer of new industrial technologies, you may find these technologies revealed in the centuries-old craft traditions of working with the materials offered by the environment to create a traditional mobile, practical, insulated approach to dwelling. The lightness and agility of Inuit kayaks, the symmetry and insulation of an expertly constructed igloo, the precision and balance of a harpoon head, or the sensual feel of the snow through the sole of waterproof sealskin boots: these are interpreted as expressions of a more embodied sense of autonomy that has existed in harmony with the environment, and has been tested and proven over time. Ironically this is in fact a very conservative understanding of autonomy that is at odds with the Inuit fascination for experimenting with technologies.

It is curious that while Inuit young and old enjoy both craft-based and industrial technologies, many thoughtful outside observers—journalists, explorers, and anthropologists—tend to privilege the traditional craft knowledge as authentic over and above technologies of industrial origin, which are largely ignored or dismissed as though they were merely

1
Simon Schaffer, "Enlightened Automata," William Clark et al., *The Sciences in Enlightened Europe* (Chicago and London, 1999), pp. 126–65; Otto Mayr, *Authority, Liberty, and Automatic Machinery in Early Modern Europe*, 1st ed. (Baltimore, 1989); Marshall Berman, *All That Is Solid Melts into Air: The Experience of Modernity* (New York, 1988).

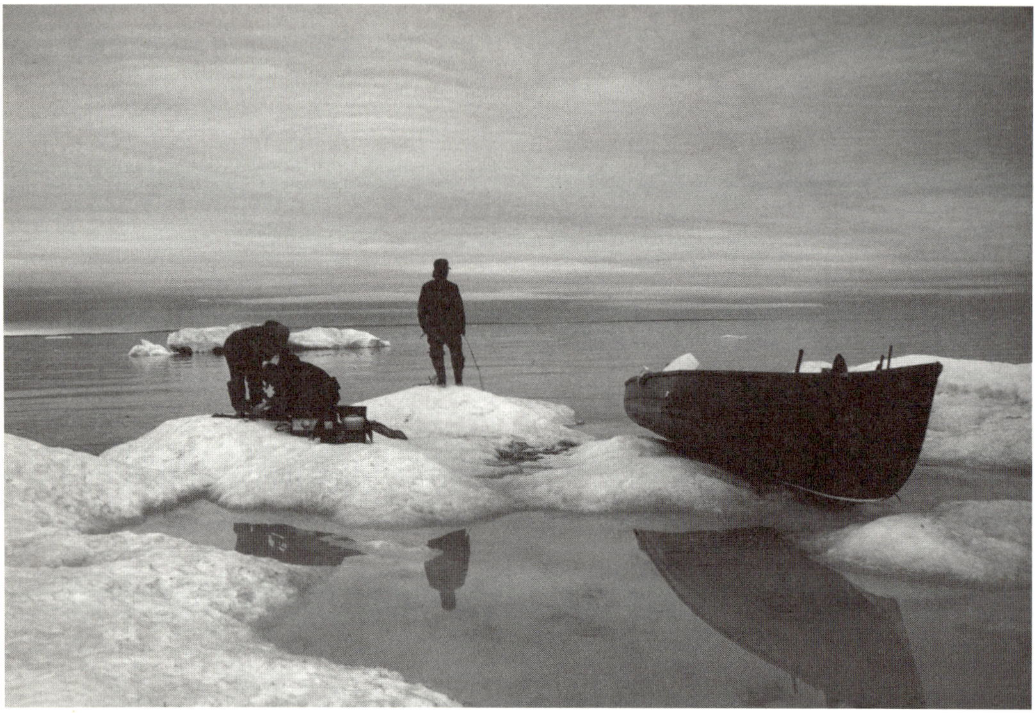

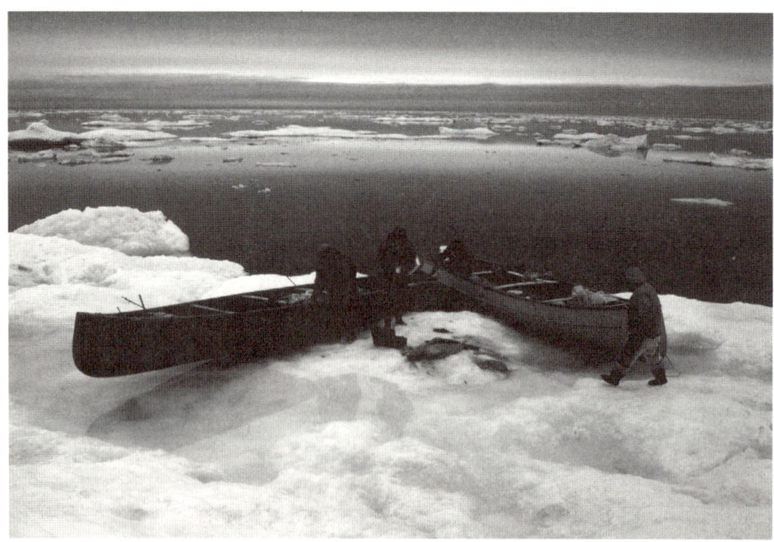

Arctic Passage: Inuit "canoes" hauled up on the sea ice after a morning of navigation and hunting. Photo: Michael Bravo, Igloolik, 1988.

Arctic Homeland: packing up after lunch on the sea ice.
Photo: Michael Bravo, Igloolik, 1988.

superficial and not engrained within the culture itself. However, my Inuit friends do not feel any less traditional in their identity on account of using snowmobiles and outboard engines; on the contrary, those who can afford them, crucially, have far greater mobility and access to the traditional camps where long-term family memory, spirits, and tradition are situated. Industrial technologies are essential for sustaining traditional aspects of identity.

On my reading, the popular interest in traditional Inuit technology sits perfectly alongside traditional Inuit interest in industrial technology. This suggests to me that technological fetishism can find expression in very different kinds of autonomous masculinity that are asymmetrically linked. Maybe "gadgets and gear" are a way of breaking the ice in a cross-cultural conversation, something like a "Berlitz guide" for getting around in another culture. Those of us who find autonomy in our own lives through cars, PCs, mobile phones, the electricity grid, etc., seem to be fascinated by the "nomadic" gear of a traditional hunting society. Is this because we recognize something of our cultural selves in them, a bridge to the culture of other men? Perhaps we fall into the classic trap of a romantic and constructed sense of our own humanity's deep history? Or perhaps this speaks to a deep masculine fear that when our own way of life totally disintegrates and we are survivors in a world like that described by Cormac McCarthy in *The Road*, the ultimate specialists in self-sufficiency will be the ones with the autonomy to soldier on. Now, as it happens, indigenous peoples of the Arctic all tell us that survival is the result of social connectedness and not skill *per se;* being an isolated individual, no matter how talented, is the certain road to death.[2]

What lies behind this appetite for "trading down" from the industrial to the artisanal, from the autonomy of living in a globalized world of complex industrial systems to a different autonomy that comes from self-reliance and skillfulness?

The apparent recognition of *verisimilitude* in skill and technology across cultures has a significant history that can help us to unlock the wider story about the role of gender in cross-cultural technological interventions and conversations. Nineteenth-century Arctic explorers in general jumped at the opportunity to try their hands at igloo-building or driving dog teams when encountering Inuit communities. Early twentieth-century polar explorers repeatedly drew on, borrowed, and transplanted the techniques of northern indigenous peoples with dogs, sleds, caribou parkas, in executing their heroic tests of masculine strength on expeditions employed at both ends of the earth for explicitly geopolitical aims. By the nineteen-thirties, kayaking was becoming a regular pastime on Arctic expeditions. Postwar kayaking grew into a popular activity together with canoeing. There is plenty of evidence then to show that the wider

2
Cormac McCarthy, *The Road* (New York, 2006).

enthusiasm for these Inuit technologies has been anything but casual. Inuit technologies have permeated the geopolitical expansionist goals of nation-states and have found a home at the core of middle-class recreation in northern countries.

Skill as a Cross-Cultural Vocabulary

The historian Michael Adas has argued that the West has used its modern advantages in technological development to construct a dialogical divide between the West and the Rest.[3] This is congruent with Edward Said's thesis in *Orientalism* that the orient is primarily an act of literary and cultural imagination defined by binary oppositions like masculine/feminine, dominant/submissive, and rational/intuitive.[4] The considerable scholarship that has since looked at Said's work usefully reminds us that the way cross-cultural communication is framed, using literary devices together with its aesthetic appeal, is in fact structured by geopolitical relations of asymmetry and inequality. That observation is highly pertinent to this discussion.

In the geopolitics of exploration, the cross-cultural pairings of technologies like the whaling ship and the kayak are framed by spatial politics in which cultures have been historically classified by technology, economics, and scale, as I shall go on to explain. Consider other pairings like the field station/house and the igloo; the rifle and the harpoon/spear; Goretex extreme-weather clothing and caribou parkas. The pairings make sense because of a notion of shared function and because of a supposed contrast between artisanal and industrial cultures. The Inuit technologies and skills that are the most collectable mirror the Western gaze, and are those most strongly associated with hunting activities.

That is certainly not to say that Inuit women are any less skillful than the men. The control, knowledge, work, and self-discipline required for preparing and sewing sealskin to make a waterproof boot *(kamik)* or a caribou skin into a winter *parka* requires knowledge and skill of the very highest order—and the expertise of some of the northern indigenous peoples was brought together and showcased by the British Museum in an exhibition entitled *Annuraaq—Arctic Clothing from Igloolik* (2001) curated by a team led by Jonathan King.[5] Moreover it is seldom appreciated that a small minority of Inuit women have been accomplished hunters in their own right. However, this is not to be confused with the cultural politics of cross-cultural pairing or verisimilitude that I believe is closely linked to the valorization of hunting.

The gender of the indigenous Inuit hunter as represented in exploration and travel writing exists in tension: masculine by virtue of possessing rational qualities and the power of precise judgment like the explorer and soldier, but female by virtue of

3
Michael Adas, *Machines as the Measure of Men: Science, Technology, and Ideologies of Western Dominance* (Ithaca, 1990).
4
Edward W. Said, *Orientalism* (New York, 1978).

5
Jonathan King et al., *Arctic Clothing of North America: Alaska, Canada, Greenland* (Montreal, 2005).

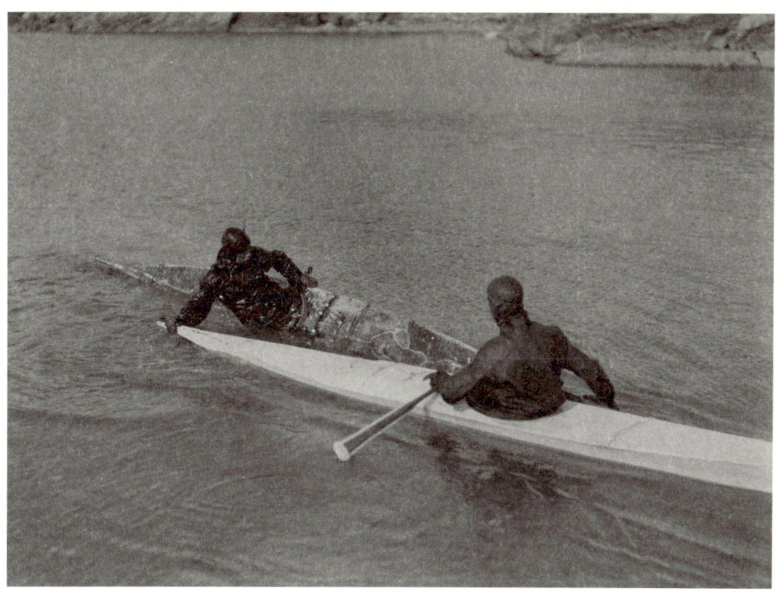

"Recovering from a Rolling Kayak," British Arctic Air Route Expeditions, 1930–31.
Kayaking was the subject of dozens of photographs by Gino Watkins's expedition
reflecting the fascination and joy they derived from the skills of this Inuit technology.
Photo: Henry Iliffe Cozens / Scott Polar Research Institute

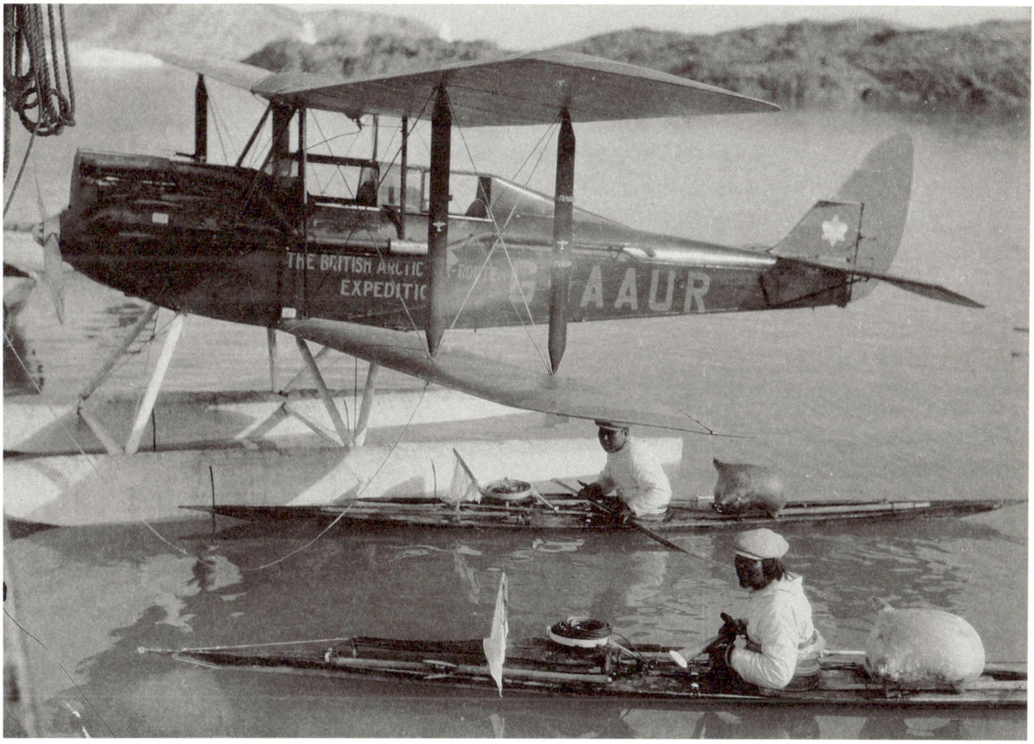

The two Greenlanders posing with their Kayaks alongside an Expedition Aircraft plays up
the idea of the expedition witnessing a technological encounter between tradition and
modernity. Photo: Alfred Stephenson / Scott Polar Research Institute

a submissive relationship to the male gaze of the gentleman ethnographic observer. And, of course, this characterization of gender is too crude, but I hope it suffices here to illustrate my argument about its importance. Following the work of Lisa Bloom and others, we now recognize that gender in exploration entails a multiplicity of historical roles and relationships, particularly where sexuality, exchange, and translation come together to generate specific orders of trust and intimacy in cross-cultural communication.[6]

It is worth pausing to understand why indigenous peoples' traditions and livelihoods are so badly served by the ways in which categories of technology are routinely employed in geopolitical discourses. Political power is associated with particular large-scale systems of transportation and communication. Following Joseph Nye, I borrow the term "technological sublime" to refer to the particular set of masculine qualities associated with the use of technological rationality to produce spatial control over great distances. Nineteenth-century trans-continental railways or twenty-first century container ships are good examples.

When we examine the cultural categories and hierarchies that inflect technological systems with meanings of power and gender, we can begin to appreciate why certain long-distance technologies belonging to indigenous traditions are often— wrongly—assumed to be local or parochial. Paradoxically Inuit technologies are admired for their extraordinary mobility over great distances, and yet they are largely considered irrelevant in geopolitics, which is a discipline with roots in the spatial politics of peoples and nations. To understand more clearly how apparently analogous kinds of skills are valued differently across a cultural divide, we need to take a step back to see the historical forces that have shaped ideas of culture, value, and exchange.

The rituals of the naval officer learning to handle indigenous canoes or other vessels, and the indigenous hunter visiting the explorer's ship were complex acts of communication and reciprocity—this was clearly understood by explorers, from James Cook in the South Seas (1766–1779) through to William Parry in the Arctic (1818–1827). The journals of explorers of the European Enlightenments are infused by discussions of this reciprocity because it was so crucial to building and evaluating degrees of mutual trust in the societies they were visiting. Trying out each other's watercraft, tools, and weapons were opportunities to build trust and confidence, to gain a measure of another society, and to calibrate the presence of the other on their respective maps. Moreover, when trust was breached, as sometimes happened, miscalculations about the purpose, display, speed, and maneuverability of small indigenous craft in some cases exacted a violent toll on the survey vessels moored offshore.

6
Lisa Bloom, *Gender on Ice: American Ideologies of Polar Expeditions* (Minneapolis, 1993).

Let's take a closer look at the tacit language of skill. The anthropologist Tim Ingold has invited us to think of skill as possessing an *interiority* in contrast to technology as knowledge being defined by *exteriority;* that is to say, knowledge that belongs to formal, rule-based systems. The politics of Ingold's distinction are rooted in a critical analysis of the Industrial Revolution. Therein lies the geopolitical imagination: the machinery of capital expropriates spatial inequalities in the distribution of labor, it dominates and forces out the ownership of skill found in the artisans; subsequently it romanticizes craft knowledge through the lens of nostalgia. The skill put on display in craft reenactments is there to show us who we are by virtue of what we no longer require of our industrialized selves.

The art of kayaking is embodied in a paddler's feel for the water translated from his body through the supple skin frame of the kayak to the water, as well as through the extension and balance given to the body provided by the force and movement of the paddle. These skills are acquired through observation, mimicry, and trial and error, not by reading a set of instructions. On the other hand, many observers and collectors of ethnographic objects have instead or also focused on the external design and structural qualities of artifacts such as a particular kayak: its weight, overall length, beam, draft, materials, and specific variations attributable to ethnicity and local customs. The contrast between the interiority and exteriority of skill offers a generic account of the fundamental difference in the way Inuit and explorers understood the same material culture that we call "kayaking." The explorers could shift from the inside to the kayaking to the outside, positioning kayaks comparatively alongside other kinds of indigenous craft in their schemas or "maps of mankind." Is that the whole story? Crucially, the autonomy implicit in mastery of one's craft is inflected by the experience of encountering others' framings of skill.

In scientific field experiments, when two parties exchange performances, techniques, or feats of skill, they are trying to map each other's skills in relation to their own, simultaneously calibrating their tacit gestural knowledge in relation to their mutual understanding and trust. They are, in fact, seeking to bridge their interior understandings of skill. Officer training in the Royal Navy, for instance, was also acquired largely through apprenticeship *in situ* and, to a much lesser extent, from navigation schools. Having a highly developed embodied capacity to read the wind and the sea was crucial—but more important was a comparable embodied knowledge of how to maintain discipline and cohesion in a ship's crew.

In my view, this goes to the heart of the cross-cultural masculinity associated with trying to emulate skilled performances with hunting technologies. It speaks to a presumed common ground that is sharply at odds with the external meanings attached to the objects in their utterly different technological systems. Kayaks for Inuit are part of a social economy of finding and sharing food across the extended family networks joined by routes across their territories. For members of the Cambridge Arctic Air Expedition, the technique of kayaking, recorded in literally dozens of photographs, appears to have been a desire to share and understand traditional Inuit skill at precisely the historical moment when explorers' reliance on such surface-based technologies appeared to be giving way to the superior power of aviation.

Technologies like kayaks and igloos have proved so important in spatial politics because, for statesmen, geographers, and ethnographers, these have been consistently adopted as markers of a masculine, and hence a putatively autonomous and objective, rendering of a culture's capability. This became a means of linking the classification of geopolitical power and the ethnographic classification of technological power. These classificatory schema (e.g., evolutionary progress) provided an index or scale against which artifacts could stand in as markers of the progress of peoples. Ethnographic comparisons and judgments were part of the lingua franca of the politics of colonies and frontiers.[7] Actually this was just as true of precision scientific instruments that served as an index of intellectual power among European states (e.g., rivalry between Germany, France, and England at world fairs). Comparisons of tools and weapons purchased, bartered, or stolen from indigenous peoples were similarly discussed and debated by men of science (e.g., Inuit vs. Aborigines of Australia). Of course, the same kinds of classificatory index were used to construct tables showing the relative divisions between the peoples of industrialized nation-states possessing technology and those societies that were perceived (often wrongly) to be nomadic tool users lacking political institutions. The criteria for indexing peoples changed over time, but they served a constant pedagogical purpose, teaching their audiences that there is a spatial order distinguishing the peoples and nations of the world. Politics, technology, and ethnography could all be submitted to measurement and division. Actually similar logics of classification are ubiquitous today, infecting elite and popular cultures. They abound in our everyday vocabulary of ethnicity and entitlement.

Peripheries are often good places from which to think differently about spatial orders and hierarchies. In her ongoing study of community-based thinking about governance, Jackie Price has argued that Inuit spatial principles of orientation used at traditional camps may be just as applicable to her experience of life in Nunavut's communities or towns. Moreover, it is a mistake to imagine that communities are bounded and divorced from the space of the land and sea around them. Taking up her insight, we might agree then that there is no *a priori* reason

7
"Technologies of Indigeneity: Measuring the Danes and Eskimos," in *Narrating the Arctic: A Cultural History of Nordic Scientific Practices,* ed. Michael Bravo and Sverker Sörlin (Canton, MA, 2002), pp. 235–73; George Stocking, ed., *Objects and Others: Essays on Museums and Material Culture*, 1st ed. (Madison, 1988).

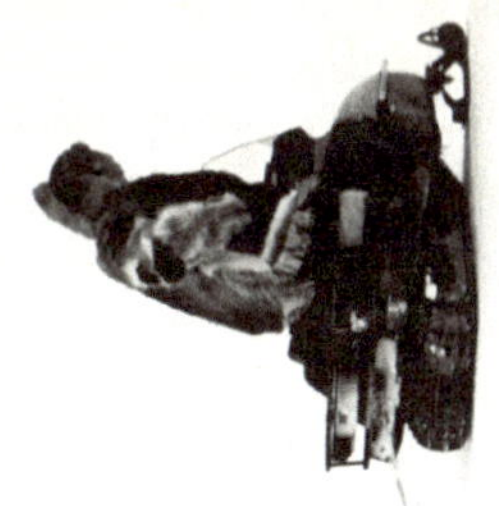

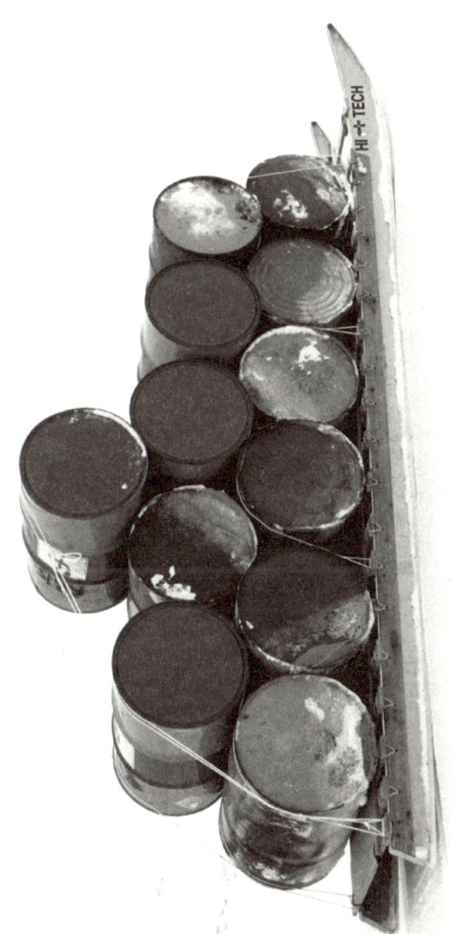

Inuit hunter hauling oil drums on a sled.
Photo: Paul Nicklen / National Geographic Image Collections

why Inuit should believe that being able to kayak counts as a stand against modernity or a defense of the space of traditional culture. Equally, there is no reason to suppose that a kayak equipped with GPS, satellite Internet access, and an array of environmental monitoring sensors is any less traditional than one without them.[8] The greatest obstacles to experimenting with—let's call it the "open source kayak"—are the formidable layers of historical sedimentation that still tell us this "must be wrong" and unfaithful to Inuit values! The impressive record of indigenous peoples in making cultural and political interventions across the grain of dominant geopolitical categories is itself an argument against a theory of geopolitics based on rigid or discrete prescribed hierarchies of scales and levels.

In one sense the Arctic Perspective Initiative is all about autonomous masculinity with the love of communications gear —but with a difference! Marko Peljhan's work, starting with his Makrolab project and building up to his present collaboration with Matthew Biederman in the Arctic Perspective Initiative, is designed precisely to bypass and therefore subvert the classificatory histories that tell people where they stand in the pecking order of nations. When the artists bring to Igloolik their own Unmanned Autonomous Devices, designed in Slovenia and equipped with inexpensive arrays of sensors for environmental monitoring, their intention is to democratize the way we think as much as what we know.

To see more clearly why Igloolik is such a good place for thinking, I want to introduce two earlier examples of technological collaborations and experiments in the community. My intention here is only to illustrate aspects of opening up technology and politics, not to be comprehensive.

Two Technological Experiments at Igloolik
Experiment 1: The Research Station

The Eastern Arctic Research Center, known locally as the "Lab" or the "Snowy Owl," is visually one of the most prominent buildings in Igloolik (plate 8 p. 8). It was instigated as an experimental technology in three senses: to explore a new design for a house of experiment, to create a state platform for observing social change in Inuit society, and to cultivate science as a useful civic activity. The Lab overlooked the community while also being set apart from it. The architectural design was an experiment in modernism and an example of a trend to imagine a future Arctic with modernist "science cities." To the visitor's eye, the Lab resembles a flying saucer or a mushroom. My impression is that the feeling of surveillance derives from its height and the relative elevation of the land that slopes down toward the shoreline.

Opened by the Canadian government in 1975, its principal intended users were government and university

8
Claudio Aporta and Eric Higgs, "Satellite Culture: Global Positioning Systems, Inuit Wayfinding, and the Need for a New Account of Technology," *Current Anthropology* 46, no. 5 (2005), pp. 729–53.

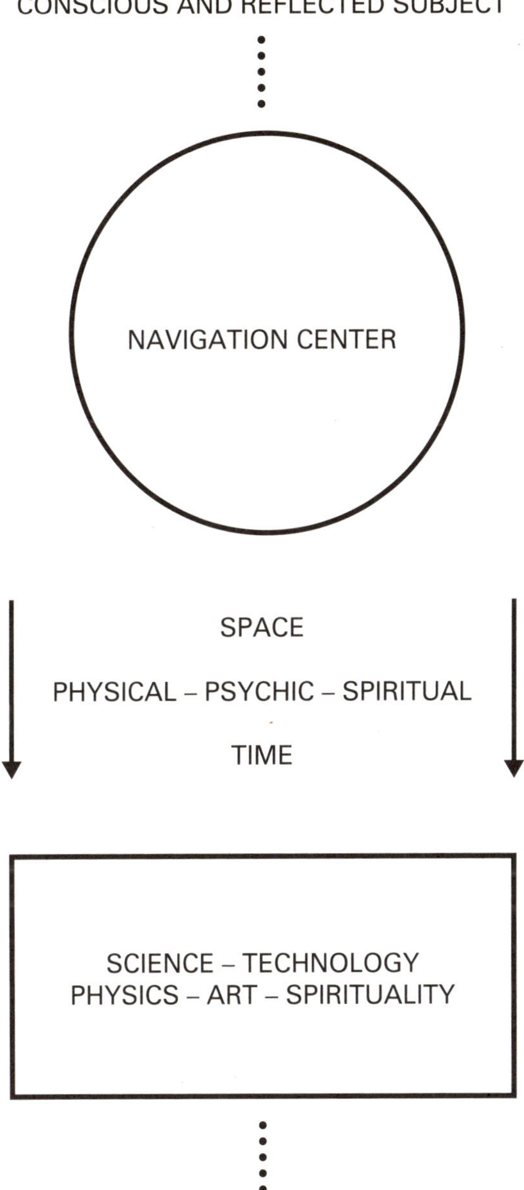

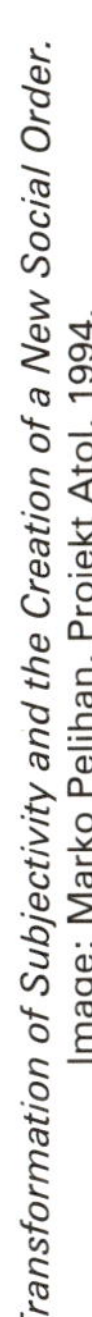

Transformation of Subjectivity and the Creation of a New Social Order.
Image: Marko Peljhan, Projekt Atol, 1994.

researchers from southern Canada, as well as student field schools. Its remit, however, also encouraged the senior resident scientist to facilitate sharing between scientists and the community. It seemed diplomatic to encourage visitors to explain what they were doing and, where possible, to show how the research could be useful for local people. Creating work for staff and guides, showing educational films for the public, communicating research results, and answering the community's questions—these were examples of ways the community could use science and technology. It was a traditional model of the "public understanding of science" with the exteriority of expert knowledge practice writ large upon the local landscape. In due course, the Lab would become an exchange house for learning, trading, and negotiating different kinds of skill through a varied set of national and international relationships.[9]

Intrigued by its design and intended function in the community, I went to visit its architect, Guy Gérin-Lajoie, at his home near Mont Tremblant in Quebec. He explained to me that he had found inspiration in the work of Ludwig Mies van der Rohe (1886–1969) (pers. comm. 2000), particularly his dedication to exploring modularity and materials. Gérin-Lajoies developed innovative, energy-efficient plastic composite materials in the form of fiberglass-reinforced polyester panels. His philosophy was a "total approach" in which modular units were made in "shapes and textures compatible with the materials."[10] The idea was that people would, one day, be able to buy room-sized units off the shelf and assemble and extend them quickly and easily along steel grids into new shapes and sizes. The panels could in principle be very quickly assembled by a small number of men in the short period of an Igloolik summer. In practice the building was constructed over two summers by a team from the community led by the first resident scientist, Andris Rode, who remembers it as a physically very demanding project.

Highly insulated and modular, the idea was to find a vernacular style to complement the community and landscape. The popular allusions to Mars suggest it didn't entirely succeed. However those working in it grew to be very affectionate about the building.

Spatially, I think the basic operational model applied to the network of the several northern research stations replicated the core–periphery model of the southern-based Arctic administration. This was transposed onto Igloolik's relationship with the regional network of trails and camps. The Lab itself was a fixed building, a scientific hub for knowledge-gathering. A sub-field outpost station at Sarcpa Lake was used mainly by student groups, but transportation was a problem. The Lab was supported by an adjacent garage stocked with a small number of trucks, snowmobiles, and all-terrain vehicles for local transport around what is a small island. Being able get off the island

9
Michael Bravo, "Science for the People: Northern Field Stations and Governmentality," *British Journal of Canadian Studies* 19, no. 2 (2006), pp. 221–45.

10
"Montreal Architect Perfects Technology of Modular Living Space," *The Citizen*, July 14, 1990, section C, p. 1.

separates those who have access to traditional camps from those who do not. Lab managers bemoaned the fact that their slim budget did not allow them to purchase a decent boat for traveling off the island during the summer, its busiest season. Of course they had none of the helicopter time available to scientists at the Polar Continental Shelf Project. The practical alternative was to make arrangements with local guides who supplied their own equipment and vehicles. Ironically, it was precisely the station's lack of autonomous mobility in its field-work that helped give the community a more significant role in the everyday practice of science. Access to the waters around Igloolik was negotiated and therefore contingent on the life and movements of community members.

The dependence of scientific research on hydrocarbons and internal combustion engines was rarely remarked upon; for decades the whole way of life in each Arctic community had depended on an annual fuel drop. Core–periphery relationships were so deeply embedded in state thinking about the Arctic that the extraordinary cost of living has too often been seen as a natural property of the Arctic without sufficient recognition that it is as much a property of the core–periphery systems of production, infrastructure, and distribution.

Electricity in Nunavut's communities is tied to diesel generators. Consequently, discussions about restricted mobil-ity and communications took the energy systems as "givens." Instead, discussions inevitably revolved around budgets, costs, and the threat of closure. Since the Lab's heating required the constant use of a diesel generator, heating accounted for the principal nonsalary component of the budget.

What makes Arctic Canada so expensive?[11] Its economy is almost totally dependent on hydrocarbons for passenger travel (airplanes), fresh supermarket food (airplanes), central heating (community-based grid with local generators), and rural mobility (snowmobiles, boats). The lion's share of profits from hydrocarbon and mineral extraction go south with only a tiny fraction supporting the tax base of the northern regional econ-omy. Add to this a small service sector economy, together with an airline monopoly, and it becomes clear that the Canadian Arctic is configured around an asymmetric economy: profits flow south, state subsidies and transfer payments flow north. Forced dependence on the state may seem like an economic sleight of hand, but it is a very tragic legacy that permeates so many aspects of people's lives. That may (in part) be why the autonomous masculinity of the Arctic is sometimes expressed through the mad freedom of driving machines to their very limits and beyond. And perhaps the Arctic Perspective Initiative has something to say about this madness.

It is no surprise that the fiscal model of scientific research for much of the Circumpolar Arctic is caught up in a tradi-

11
A general overview of Arctic economic systems is provided in Gérard Duhaime et al., "Economic systems," *AHDR (Arctic Human Development Report)* (2004), pp. 69–84.

tion of state policies that at their heart envisaged funding for community-based knowledge and research as a tax rather than as an investment. In my opinion, the remarkable successes of the Igloolik research station owed more to its carefully managed insulation (not disconnection) from the state than from the Arctic environment. Nevertheless, the vulnerability of the Arctic research networks became painfully obvious in the nineteen-nineties as the system was starved of funding and the state's investment in visiting researchers became critically reduced.[12]

The story of this research station (and many others) in Arctic Canada is that it was run on a shoestring budget, much to the credit of those individuals who managed these stations, sometimes at their own expense. What they achieved was often the product of their ingenuity and never-say-die commitment. One example succinctly illustrates the economics of Arctic research. In the mid-nineteen-nineties, professor Paul Hebert of Guelph University calculated that it would cost less to transport and run his biology field school at Cairns by the Great Barrier Reef in Australia, than to fly them to Igloolik for the same period (pers. comm. 2006). After years down under, he is now back in the North, but, closer to home, in the sub-Arctic.

And yet the much older Inuit subsistence model of hunting, trails, and camps—admittedly with its own central nodes—demonstrates that there are other viable technological systems that have been incredibly successful in managing distance in the Arctic. As David Turnbull explains in his essay, the Inuit social-cognitive-material competences enabled them to function as a resilient adaptive system and to play a part in the history of humanity's story, which began "out of Africa" and over millennia reached the Arctic.

Experiment 2: The Floe Edge Boat

The Lab's second director or manager, John MacDonald, had come to Igloolik in 1985 with a keen interest in Inuit language, culture, and art. Many of the Lab's Inuit staff, past and present —including George Qulaut, Louis Tapardjuk, Leah Otak, Paul Irngaut, and Maurice Arnatsiaq—were also attracted by a keen interest in studying Inuit traditional knowledge and have an impressive string of achievements to show for it.[13]

I asked John MacDonald to tell me about the floe edge boat project, which had been suggested to John by George Qulaut, his senior member of staff. The idea was to design a small fiberglass boat that could be used by hunters at the floe edge (where the sea ice meets the water). Hunting marine mammals at the floe edge, particularly seals, is a central part of Inuit life in late winter, spring, and early summer. Yet retrieving them from the water at the floe edge is difficult and requires skill, physical strength, speed, balance, and agility. A heavy or

---

12
John England, "Canada Needs a Polar Policy," *Nature* 463, no. 7278 (January 14, 2010), p. 159.

13
One excellent example of the work of the Igloolik Elders Project was their collaboration with John MacDonald, which led to the publication of John MacDonald, *The Arctic Sky: Inuit Astronomy, Star Lore, and Legend* (Toronto, 1988).

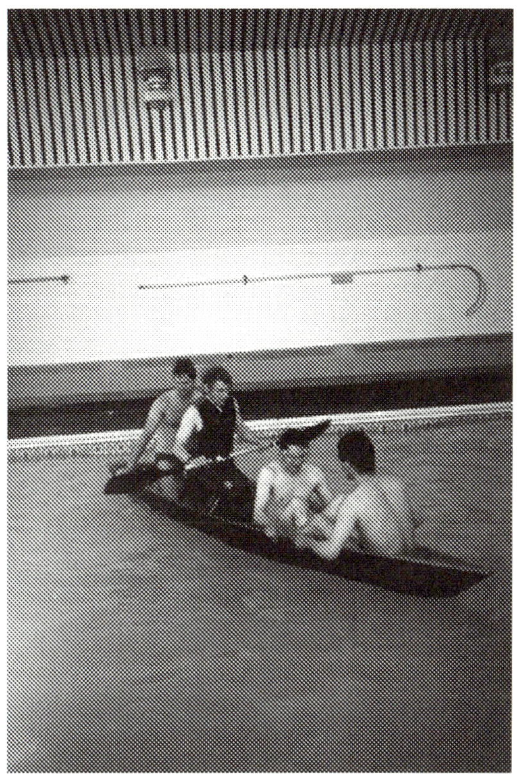

Floe edge boat experiment in the Igloolik community swimming pool to determine the seal-equivalent ballast limit of the prototype, 1985. Photo: John MacDonald

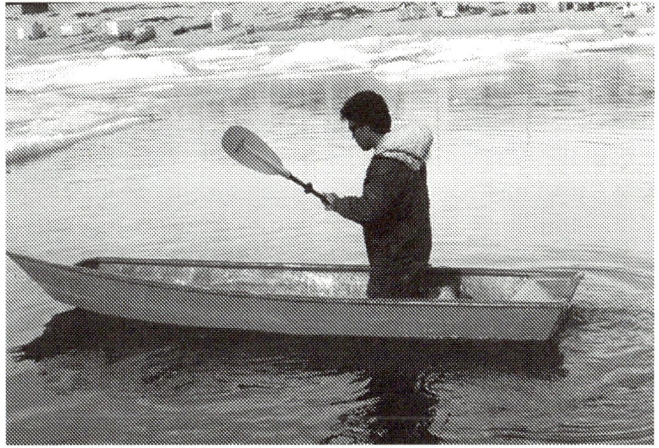

Joannie Ijjangiaq carrying out experimental maneuvers with the floe edge boat prototype near the Igloolik shoreline, 1985. Photo: John MacDonald

slippery animal can be unwieldy, cause a hunter to lose balance, or even to capsize. George explained that the plywood boats then in use were cumbersome to maneuver. The reader needs to imagine a hunter who, having managed to kill a seal, has to pull the seal up and over the gunwale, come alongside the edge of the ice (of some thickness), get out of the boat, and then haul the boat and the animal onto the ice—not so easily done! In a situation like that, there are design trade-offs between a boat's stability, size, shape, and maneuverability.

The Lab staff found partners in Victor Aqatsiaq and Cain Iqqaqsaq, members of senior standing at the Igloolik Hunters and Trappers Association (HTA). After testing two prototypes, they started small-scale production. The HTA was given the mold and basic manufacturing training for their staff. Each boat was essentially handmade and required about four days' work. Boats were purchased and orders began also coming in from the neighboring communities of Arctic Bay and Pond Inlet. Subsequently the project was showcased at Expo 86 in Vancouver.

Part of the project's initial appeal for the Lab was that it fulfilled its "technology transfer brief." MacDonald was himself a recreational sea-kayaking enthusiast. Likeminded friends had persuaded Nordkapp in northern Norway to send a mold to Iqaluit to see whether Inuit might constitute a new emerging market for (fiberglass) kayaks! Having tried his hand at producing some Nordkapp kayaks, MacDonald brought his experience to the floe edge boat project. The HTA added their tacit knowledge and experience of floe edge boats to this marriage of experimental practice. The Igloolik swimming pool was used for the laboratory phase of testing. The photograph on page 53 shows the team simulating the buoyancy of a loaded boat by adding passengers (in place of a seal). This was critical because the hunters wanted a very low freeboard (i.e., the height of the gunwales above the water) to make it simpler to load the catch. The team constructed two prototypes, one with a symmetrical bow and stern, and a second with dropped stern to enable a hunter to pull a seal on board at the waterline (ill. p. 53). The team played with the design, modifying the shape of the mold, adding a central keel and two parallel rail keels either side. (Nordkapp enthusiasts and other readers wanting to produce a similar design are recommended to place the rail keels about ten inches either side of the central keel for optimal stability and performance.)

It is strange that floe edge boats have not become a regular feature of the Igloolik shoreline. Why did production of the floe edge boat not really take off after its initial successes and acclaim? After all, this seems like a perfect example of an experiment in using new materials to improve an existing traditional technology—a pattern repeated time and again by Inuit over the centuries with wood, iron, and plastic. There is no obvious answer except that the HTA lacked the institutional will to undertake the production on a commercial basis. I have also sometimes observed that scaling up successful experiments of any kind is a difficult challenge in Nunavut because of the relative lack of local experience in raising capital and implementing economic development projects.

Conclusion

Earlier in the essay I introduced the idea that skill can be understood as a gestural language with a capacity for shared tacit meanings that can bridge what are otherwise radically different cultural perspectives. Skill in the field sciences is normally embodied as experimental practice. Yet even the most esoteric skills like the use of navigation instruments lend themselves to a wide range of symbolic spatial performances. The floe edge boat exemplifies this reading of skill perfectly. As John MacDonald described to me the experiments with the prototypes in the Igloolik swimming pool and on the beach, I could see the interplay of many elements that historians tell us are characteristics of experimentation between the laboratory (station, garage, and swimming pool) and the field (beach, floe edge): bricolage, iteration, trial and error, messiness, self-discipline, demonstration, precision, measurement, replication, humor, and imagination. Which of these qualities were highlighted when the boat was displayed and described at Expo 86 in Vancouver would be interesting to know. In general, an expo is a textbook example of displaying indigenous skill and ingenuity that grew out of the nineteenth-century tradition of world's fairs—exhibitions whose purpose was to host large displays of nations' achievements in industry, innovation, and the arts.

Though it seems too bad that the floe edge boat, today, is more of a forgotten artifact or a museum piece than living technology being used all over Nunavut to haul seals onto the ice floe, it is easy to lose sight of the boat's greater significance. It illustrates the capacity of the Igloolik community to work with the Lab to mobilize international construction technologies to produce new knowledge and designs to meet their own needs. It is actually one of many examples of how the mixed indigenous-settler northern communities are knowledge-rich—arguably having a surplus of ideas and creative thinking—enabling them to build autonomy flexibly and adaptively in response to their own changing needs and priorities as they identify them. This is incredibly important to remember because people who live outside the Arctic overwhelmingly still perceive modernity as something the world *inflicts on* its geographical peripheries, a necessary if regrettable step in the march of progress for those who lack modern technology. Yet this view totally fails to recognize that indigenous societies have a long and continuous history of political and technical inventiveness.

56

Traveling through Layers: Inuit Artists Appropriate New Technologies

Katarina Soukup

When the time came a few years ago to find an Inuktitut term for the word *Internet,* Nunavut's former Official Languages Commissioner, Eva Aariak, chose *ikiaqqivik,* or "traveling through layers" (Minogue, 2005). The word comes from the concept describing what a shaman does when asked to find out about living or deceased relatives or where animals have disappeared to: travel across time and space to find answers. According to the elders, shamans used to travel all over the world: to the bottom of the ocean, to the stratosphere, and even to the moon. In fact, the 1969 moon landing did not impress Inuit elders. They simply said, "We've already been there!" (Minogue, 2005). The word is also an example of how Inuit are mapping traditional concepts, values, and metaphors to make sense of contemporary realities and technologies.

Like shamans in the digital age perhaps, Igloolik Isuma Productions (http://isuma.ca), the acclaimed Inuit media-art collective behind the award-winning feature film *Atanarjuat (The Fast Runner)* (Kunuk, 2001), employs cutting-edge technologies such as high-definition video and wireless broadband to "travel through the layers" of time, geography, language, history, and culture. Isuma's films, like the award-winning *Atanarjuat,* the thirteen-part *Nunavut (Our Land)* television series (Igloolik Isuma Productions, 1994–1995), and the feature film *The Journals of Knud Rasmussen* (Kunuk & Cohn, 2006), allow us to the see the living traditions of the past and demonstrate through their re-creation in film and video that Inuit are still able to practice them in the present. Isuma's films extend the ancient art of Inuit storytelling into the digital age through video art and filmmaking, appropriating these technologies to present to the world a discourse from a distinctly Inuit point of view and thereby combat the historical media image of the Inuk as Other. In this media report, I hope to illustrate how Isuma "travels across time" through its films and videos and "travels across space" through its work with the Internet.

Traveling across Time

In the period of a few generations, communities of Inuit throughout the North have undergone a dramatic transition from lifestyles based predominantly on nomadic subsistence hunting and fishing to a sedentary, wage-based, consumer economy. Values, traditions, and skills that had in some cases existed for thousands of years were challenged and threatened by new conditions, living arrangements, and other stressors. Starting early in the twentieth century, missionaries both promoted widespread conversion to Christianity and concomitantly devalued and stigmatized traditional religion and healing practices. Shamans and their traditional practices were denigrated and suppressed. The few shamans that continued to practice did so in a way that did not draw the attention of governmental and Christian religious authorities. In many instances, the missionaries were eventually seen by the Inuit to be replacing the shamans, and Christian beliefs and practices became widespread.

As elsewhere among Aboriginal populations in North America, young people were mandated to go to school, often in residential settings far from their original communities. These institutions facilitated further loss of cultural traditions, both through their emphasis on the values and traditions of the dominant southern culture and the active denigration of the traditions, languages, and beliefs of the Inuit culture. As the twentieth century progressed, the presence of both the federal government and the military played a greater role in the lives of the Inuit. Communities were consolidated into large settlements with residential populations sometimes numbering in the thousands, and lifestyles changed significantly in many ways. Although there is evidence of 4,000 years of continuous habitation on the island (called *Iglulik*, "or place of houses"), the settled community known today as Igloolik was created only in the last fifty years, when federal government agents coerced Inuit living in small nomadic hunting camps in the region to settle in one location as a way of more easily administering them.

Arctic scholar Robin Gedalof writes how the Inuit are "time-travelers," and ". . . are probably the only people in history ever to have made the transition from the Stone Age to the Atomic Age in one generation. . . . [They] have adjusted from an admittedly rich but primitive nomadic isolation to a life of satellite communication. They have grown up in a bone culture and have grown old driving tractor-trailers and typing out their memoirs for the benefit of millions of people . . ." (quoted in Columbo, 1997, p. 12). Indeed, Isuma's upcoming feature film documents some of these dramatic changes. *The Journals of Knud Rasmussen* (2006) is about the cultural encounter that occurred when the Danish explorer Knud Rasmussen and his Greenlandic companions passed through the Iglulik region in the nineteen-twenties during the fifth Thule expedition, a voyage by dog-team across the Arctic from Greenland to Alaska. Rasmussen's goal was to collect material, spiritual, and intellectual elements of indigenous culture in order to prove that there was a common language and culture across the Arctic (Rasmussen, 1999). Rasmussen was unique among Arctic explorers in that his grandmother was an Inuk from Greenland, he was raised in both Denmark and Greenland, and, more importantly, he spoke Inuktitut fluently.

In 1922, Rasmussen met the famous Igloolik shaman Avva and his family. He stayed with them for a period of time and collected the life stories of Avva and his wife, Orulu, before leaving for another region. This moment in time would later prove to be a turning point for Inuit in Igloolik, unleashing many of the radical changes described above. Indeed, one year later, Rasmussen returned to Iglulik and found that Avva had converted to Christianity.

While these changes are astonishing, Inuit culture and identity has nevertheless remained profoundly tied to the land. The Inuit of Igloolik, for instance, have been in regular contact with the South for over forty years, and actively incorporate southern technologies and consumer products into their everyday lives, all while renewing and reinventing "appropriated uses" that suit their needs. From this is born a contemporary aesthetic that is rarely understood or valued—since the outside world prefers the classic symbols of ancient/traditional Inuit culture associated with Otherness.

Igloolik, a remote community of 1,200 people on an island in Canada's eastern Arctic, has a long, rich history of community media production for cultural purposes. In the nineteen-seventies, Isuma cofounder Paul Apak Angilirq participated in the Inukshuk Project, an experimental federal program that trained Inuit in basic television production skills. In 1975 and again in 1979, the community of Igloolik voted against accepting satellite television, preferring instead to wait until Inuktitut-language television programming became available, which it did with the establishment of the Inuit Broadcasting Corporation (IBC) in 1982.

Paul Apak Angilirq and Zacharias Kunuk worked for IBC for a number of years before deciding to leave that organization to pursue independent media production. Their chief complaints with IBC were that the management was based in Ottawa and that they never had the budgets to make drama that could visually illustrate oral history and storytelling by the elders. In the late nineteen-eighties, the pair met New York video artist Norman Cohn at an IBC training workshop in Iqaluit, and the three, along with Igloolik elder Pauloosie Qulitallik, founded Igloolik Isuma Productions in 1990. As Canada's first Inuit independent production company, Isuma's mission is to create a distinctive Inuit style of community-based filmmaking that preserves and enhances Inuit culture, creates needed employment, and offers a uniquely Inuit point of view to the global media audience. Since 1989 Isuma's twenty-five films have won awards and critical acclaim in Canada and worldwide, including the Camera d'or at Cannes in 2001 for *Atanarjuat (The Fast Runner)*.

Isuma is known for its unique "docudrama" aesthetic, which brings forward the past and melds it into the present. In many of Isuma's earlier videos (such as the *Nunavut [Our land]* series), actors were given only a general story arc and improvised the details. As Norman Cohn points out, Isuma's docudrama is "based on people living the dramatic experience . . . Inuit historical fiction is possible because the traditional history is so close in time to contemporary life, there are still people who can live their traditional history as actors. So that instead of having to act out, having to simulate the building of a stone-house, we actually build a stone-house" (quoted in Wachowich, 1997a). In more scripted projects, such as *Atanarjuat (The Fast Runner)* and *The Journals of Knud Rasmussen*, actors often inhabit their namesakes[1] and ancestors, which Cohn describes this way: "Instead of taking an actor and putting him in a character, we take a character and put him in the actor" (quoted in Wachowich, 1997a).

For his part, Zacharias Kunuk sees Isuma's style of film-making as a way of reimagining an obliterated past:

> After the missionaries dropped their religion on us, storytelling and drum-dancing were almost banned. [Filmmaking] is one way to bring it back. And shamanism, I have never seen it. I have only heard about it. I can only imagine how it looks. One way of making it visible is to film it. Not because there is a Qallunaat [white] director telling you what to do. You just make it up. (quoted in Wachowich, 1997b)

Isuma's films and videos are always based on the oral history of the community elders. In the case of *The Journals of Knud Rasmussen,* the film's storyline is based on the events recounted in Rasmussen's writings, but as the film's codirector Norman Cohn asserts, "Those events are interpreted through an *Inuit point of view*. . . . Like looking at your reflection in the window and seeing through to the other side of the window pane" (Norman Cohn, Secretary-Treasurer, Igloolik Isuma Productions, personal communication, October 31, 2004).

Stephen Muecke, Professor of Cultural Studies at the University of Technology in Sydney, has written a great deal about how the *form* of discourse shapes our understanding of Aboriginal history: "The main problem for Aboriginal History, as I see it, is to authenticate the appropriate discourse for its transmission. At the moment the 'authentic' accounts of Aboriginal history are firmly locked in academic standard English" (1983) Isuma's unique style of docudrama counters this privileging of the written word penned by Europeans as the "authentic," "true" historical record. The films do this by appropriating communication tools to transmit an audiovisual form of Inuit oral history and storytelling to a hybrid audience: Isuma's primary goal is to delight other Inuit, and its secondary goal is to connect with a global media audience. Indeed, Cohn argues that "[Inuit] storytelling as an oral form is most compatible in contemporary form with film-making or theater" (Norman Cohn, personal communication, October 31, 2004).

Traveling across Cultures and Space

For many years these media artists in Igloolik have dreamed of how to use the Internet in Igloolik to enhance and promote

---

1

In Inuit culture, children are bonded to their ancestors through their Inuit name or namesake —*tuqlluraniq*. According to Inuit custom, children "inherit" that person's family relations along with the name. This is reflected in terms of address between people: a young child named after the deceased husband of an elder woman would call her "wife," for instance. In turn, the elder would call the child "husband."

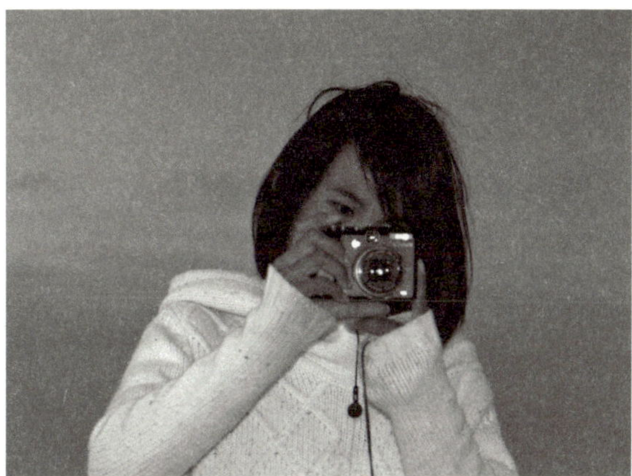

The camera is turned back on API crew member Nejc Trošt.
Igloolik, 2009. Photo: Nejc Trošt

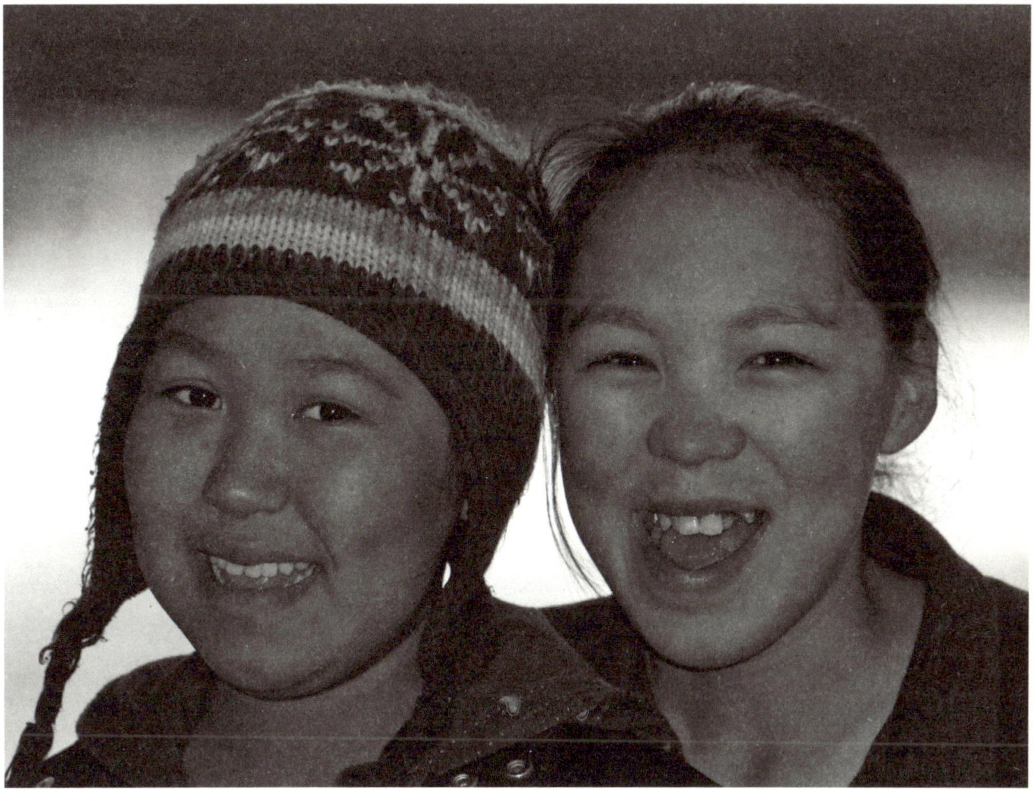

Young people of Igloolik, photo taken during API visit in 2009.
Photo: Nejc Trošt

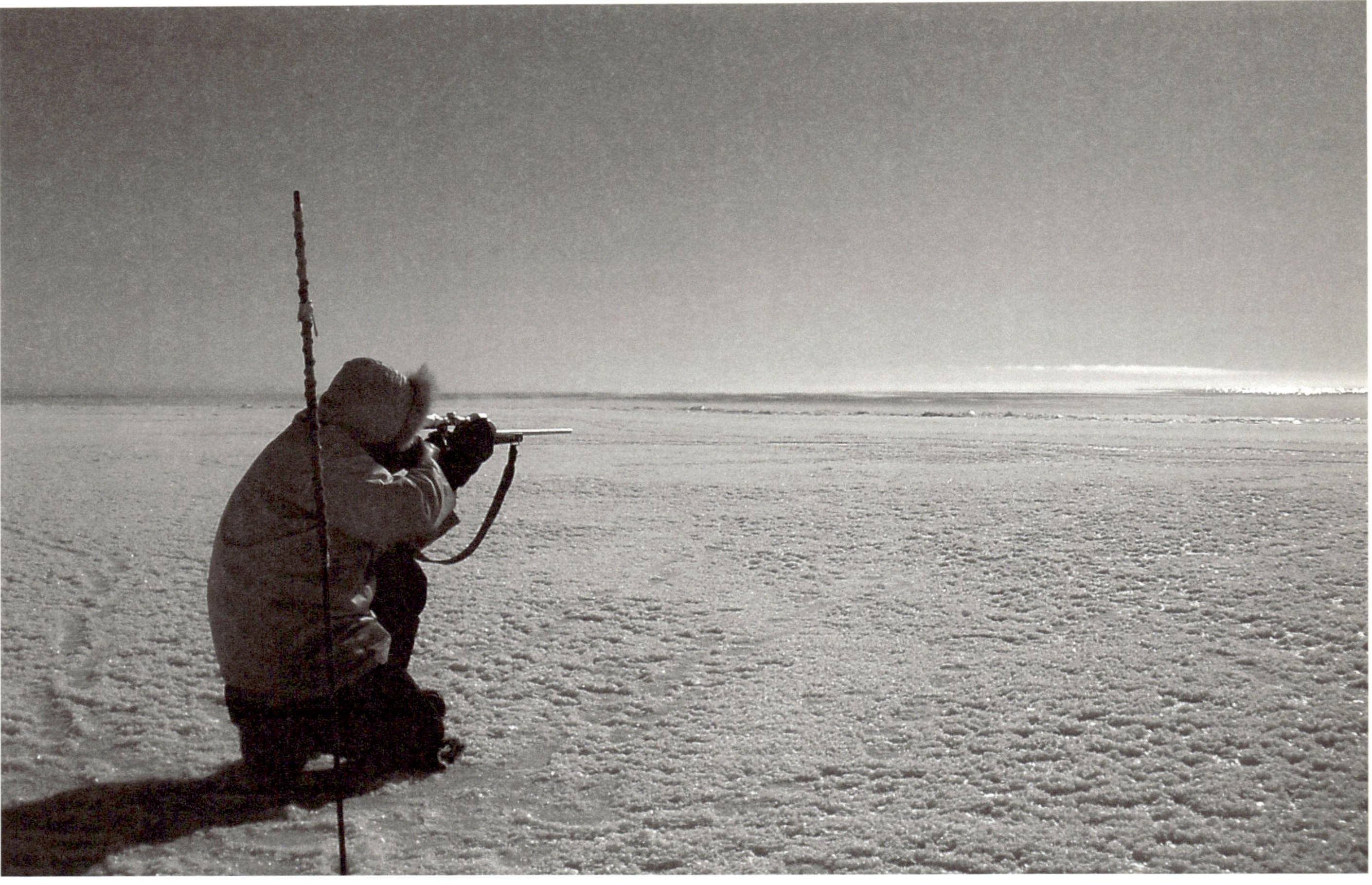

Zacharias Kunuk on the floe edge near Igloolik Island,
April 2006. Photo: API

Inuit culture as well as their own creative process. While dial-up access has been available in Nunavut for several years, it has been a slow and unstable means of connecting to the Internet, with connection speeds usually in the 14.4 kbps range that most southern Internet users last experienced a decade and a half ago.

Previous experiences using the Internet and the World Wide Web by artists in Igloolik include the experimental *Live from the Tundra* project (http://nunatinnit.org) produced by the Arnait Women's Video Workshop of Igloolik in August 2001. A group of Inuit and non-Inuit artists took a two-hour boat trip from Igloolik to a traditional Inuit outpost camp called Najuktuktujuk, far from phone and power lines. The camp was presided over by elders Enuki and Vivi Kunuk (the parents of filmmaker Zacharias Kunuk). Over five days the group uploaded daily audio, video, photo, and text dispatches to the Web from what was dubbed the Nunatinnit Mobile Media Lab, employing a high-speed data satellite phone (which at that time meant 64 kbps).

This daily journal of life in a remote outpost camp was meant to give the world a sense of the experience of living on the land in the High Arctic, as well as to push the aesthetic and technological possibilities offered by digital media and the World Wide Web—namely, hypertext, satellite technologies, streaming media, networked experiences, and mobile computing. Specifically, hypertext and integrated media permitted the expression of simultaneous, parallel, yet different experiences of the same event or moment in time (for instance, a seal hunt, sunset, walk on the land, performance, discussion, etc.). Thus, the same story or account of an experience may be told from different points of view (Inuit, southern, elder, youth, male, female, etc.) and through different media (sound, video, photo, drawing, text, etc.).

While a successful experiment in remote, mobile computing, the satellite phone technology used for *Live from the Tundra* was exorbitantly expensive (airtime alone cost U.S.$10 per minute, never mind the cost of the phone terminal itself). It did, however, give Igloolik artists such as Zacharias Kunuk the desire to explore the possibility of one day establishing a permanent mobile media lab out on the land, in a traditional camp outside the community of Igloolik, streaming their media art to the rest of the world through the Internet (Soukup, 2001).

The rollout of wireless broadband in every community throughout Nunavut in 2005, thanks to the efforts of the non-profit Nunavut Broadband Development Corporation (http://www.nunavut-broadband.ca), now makes cultural uses of the Internet far more interesting (and affordable). It may also be as revolutionary to the economic and cultural thread of the Arctic as the launch of satellite communication across Northern Canada in the nineteen-seveties—or even more so. Broadband can accommodate media-rich content, such as audio and video streaming, and thus a departure from text-based Web interaction, which is especially appropriate for a culture based on an oral language like Inuktitut (the language only came into written form less than 100 years ago, with the introduction of the syllabic writing system by Christian missionaries). Beyond cultural uses, broadband also brings great potential for distance learning, e-commerce for Nunavut's artists and craftspeople, and distance-medicine for a small population spread across a vast territory. Wireless capacity makes Internet accessible outside of the communities within a radius of thirty kilometers, meaning that Inuit will be able to use this form of communication from their hunting camps if they wish.

Isuma's goal is to find a way through wireless broadband for Inuit artists to return to a thoroughly contemporary nomadism that does not seek to throw Inuit back into the Stone Age, but instead marries tradition with the modern: remaining out on the land, living a traditional life of hunting and gathering, all while being in contact with the rest of the twenty-first century through the Internet. In Isuma's case, this means making films and television outside of the confines of town, in the beauty of the Arctic landscape where the company's films are shot, and having a remote media lab at Siuraajuk, the ancestral home of Zacharias Kunuk's family. This traditional hunting camp, about three hours by skidoo over the frozen sea ice, was the location for Isuma's feature film, *The Journals of Knud Rasmussen* (2006). For Zacharias Kunuk, who would consider himself a hunter before calling himself a filmmaker, the appeal of this "outpost camp media lab" is obvious: "being able to edit a movie, take email, and if you see a seal in the bay, you drop everything and go out after it" (Zacharias Kunuk, President, Igloolik Isuma Productions, personal communication, August 27, 2001).

In fall 2003, Isuma began developing SILA (http://www.sila.nu), an e-learning website about Inuit culture, based on its current and future films and videos. In Inuktitut, the word *sila* means "atmosphere, the outside, temperature, weather, the world." It is the dominant force in the Canadian Arctic, even in today's modern world. Nature and the vagaries of weather still trump modern technology in the Arctic. Funded by Telefilm Canada's New Media Fund, SILA represents Isuma's first large-scale new-media project.

In the development process for SILA, Isuma consulted Inuit elders to understand traditional Inuit ways of learning and teaching, and these have been incorporated into the website activities and modules. The website lesson plans also adapt and incorporate elements of Education Nunavut's innovative new curriculum based on *Inuit Qaujimajatuqangit* (IQ) (Nunavut Department of Education, 2003). IQ is defined as the Inuit way of doing things and the past, present, and future knowledge, experience, and values of Inuit society. The pedagogical framework and guiding or foundational principles are based on the essential elements of humaneness, collaboration, environmental stewardship, acquiring skills and knowledge, being resourceful to solve problems, achieving consensus in decision-making, and serving the common good. IQ values creativity and innovation in all of these essential elements, as well as in the discipline of the arts, to recognize the importance of creative expression in Inuit life and the value of artistic excellence as a way of interpreting and sharing culture and values. Isuma strongly believes that the core values and foundational principles of an IQ pedagogy will have meaning and significance to teachers and students of both Inuit and non-Inuit backgrounds. Like Isuma's films, the website is designed for a dual audience.

The biggest challenge in creating the website was to transpose Isuma's collaborative, community-based filmmaking style to the Web. At the core of SILA was the design and programming of an online collaborative space for creating content from different, remote locations, and also for those with or without much knowledge of Web design to contribute and work together. Behind SILA is a high-performance open source infrastructure, which allows for dynamic content management in real time. This authoring tool enables users with different access levels to contribute content through a very simple Web interface. Text, audio, video, and images are stored in a database, dynamically displayed and instantly available online.

Muecke (1984) also suggests a multitextual and collaborative approach to documenting Aboriginal history, one that neither privileges one point of view (non-Aboriginal) nor entrenches the dominance of the written word (most often English). Multiple forms of discourse can therefore represent a historical account. In much this vein, "Live from the Set" (http://sila.nu/live), the online production journal that chronicled the six-week shoot of the *The Journals of Knud Rasmussen,* attempted to capture this diversity of cultures and points of view, as well as document an Inuit style of filmmaking. The collaborative authoring tool developed for SILA was first used to produce "Live from the Set." The site featured video, audio, and hundreds of photographs produced by a crew of both Inuit and non-Inuit, as well as written blogs from ethno-historian Nancy Wachowich (University of Aberdeen), Inuit writer Jobie Weetaluktuk, and Isuma's own "embedded journalist,"[2] S. F. Said, a film critic with the *London Daily Telegraph*, who followed the entire filming process from first shot to production wrap. The goal of the website was to create a space on the Web that would open up a cross-cultural dialogue and intersubjective exchanges between contemporary Inuit life and culture and the outside world, between different aesthetic visions, and between different media (audio, video, text, image). In the hypertextual environment of

2
This playfully refers to the term used to refer to journalists who were attached to a military unit involved in an armed conflict during the 2003 invasion of Iraq.

the Web, these disparate visions could exist simultaneously, even in contradiction. Another way in which Isuma appropriates this new technology for literally traveling across space, to compress vast expanses of geography, is by allowing the world public to connect directly with Inuit artists and the Arctic environment. Considering that forty years ago, traveling to this region of the Arctic was only possible by ship (and took many, many months), and even today is only accessible by air (a return economy plane ticket to Igloolik costs in the order of $3,000), Igloolik is still extremely remote and difficult to visit by conventional means.

In the future, Isuma will join forces with other artists and Igloolik-based Nunavut Independent Television Network (NITV; http://nitv.nu) to stream live video and video-on-demand from the community, as well as to interact with other communities in Nunavut and around the world through video conferencing. Isuma is also collaborating with international projects such as Slovene artist Marko Peljhan's Makrolab (http://makrolab.ljudmila.org/current), an autonomous, mobile media-arts lab that was planned to be installed in Nunavut for Polar Year 2007.[3]

Isuma's videos, films, and Internet projects demonstrate how a community can appropriate communication tools to serve their own cultural, aesthetic, and linguistic purposes of Inuit culture. These audiovisual representations also enable Canadians to connect more directly with the images and their Inuit creators, and to establish a distinct and authentic Inuit voice within a global media discourse.

3
The original plans to install Makrolab in Nunavut have since evolved into the Arctic Perspective Initiative.

References

Arnait Video Productions, *Live from the Tundra:* Streaming media website from a remote outpost on Baffin Island, http://nunatinnit.org (accessed January 31, 2006).

Atanarjuat (The Fast Runner): Official website, URL: http://www.atanarjuat.com (accessed January 31, 2006).

John Columbo Robert, ed., *Poems of the Inuit* (Ottawa, 1997) (Originally published in 1981).

Robin Gedalof, *An Introduction to Canadian Eskimo Prose in English*, unpublished master's thesis (University of Western Ontario, 1977).

Igloolik Isuma Productions, *Nunavut (Our land)* [13-part television series], Canada, 1994–1995.

Inuit Broadcasting Corporation, History of the Inuit Broadcasting Corporation, http://www.inuitbroadcasting.ca/english/history.html (accessed January 31, 2006).

Zacharias Kunuk (Director), *Atanarjuat (The Fast Runner)* [Film] (Canada, 2001).

Zacharias Kunuk & Norman Cohn (Directors), *The Journals of Knud Rasmussen* [Film] (Canada & Denmark, 2006).

Sara Minogue, "Inuktitut Computing Takes Shape," *Nunatsiaq News*, July 8, 2005, http://www.nunatsiaq.com/archives/50708/news/nunavut/50708_09.html (accessed January 31, 2006).

Stephen Muecke, "Discourse, History, Fiction: Language and Aboriginal History," *Australian Journal of Cultural Studies* 1, no. 1 (May 1983), pp. 71–79.

Stephen Muecke, "How Shall We Write History?" in Krim Benterrak et al., *Reading the Country* (Fremantle, Western Australia, 1984).

Nunavut Department of Education, *Inuit Qaujimajatuqangit Schools: A New Philosophy for Education in Nunavut* (unpublished policy paper, Arviat, NU), 2003.

Knud Rasmussen, *Across Arctic America: Narrative of the Fifth Thule Expedition* (Fairbanks, 1999).

Katarina Soukup, interview with Zacharias Kunuk (audio file, August 27, 2001), http://www.nunatinnit.org/en/live/sound_list.html?id=13# (accessed January 31, 2006).

Nancy Wachowich, unpublished interview with Norman Cohn, 1997.

Nancy Wachowich, unpublished interview with Zacharias Kunuk, 1997.

Trails and Tales: Multiple Stories of Human Movement and Modernity

David Turnbull

> We speak with certainty without accepting exclusive truths. Knowledge for the Indian person is something that comes from within the person and the community. It arises from consensus. Movement is part of us. Explanations are not necessary—only stories which remind, acknowledge, and honour the power and the force of movement. People have moved from place to place and have joined and separated again through out our past, and we have incorporated it in our songs, stories, and myths because we must continually remember that without movement there is no life.[1]

1

Tessie Naranjo, "Thoughts on Migration by Santa Clara Pueblo," *Journal of Anthropological Archaeology* 14 (1995), pp. 247–250.

This is a story about the stories we tell of human movement out of Africa and around the world. It's stories at three levels, or maybe it's stories all the way down. To be able to move, to extend ourselves in space and time, we have to tell stories to persuade our trusted companions to accompany us, and to establish networks of connection. In moving we leave trails, markers of our passing, just like the animals that, in the past, we may have been tracking. We follow and describe those trails, and in the process create another set of trails and stories—cognitive trails, trails reflecting our cultural and disciplinary backgrounds, our practices, and our understandings. These stories are in turn the feedstock of the narratives of human prehistory and movements out of Africa. Narratives that, as Donna Haraway points out, naturalize understandings of the human condition and its possibilities.[2] They are among the most formative materials from which we create human identities and relations, geopolitics and autonomy. It is important, therefore, to find ways of retelling those narratives which in the past have largely supported Western hegemony and marginalized alternative ways of being, knowing, and moving.

2

Donna Haraway, *Simians, Cyborgs and Women: The Reinvention of Nature* (London, 1991).

Bacteria, pigs, rats, pots, plants, words, bones, stones, earrings, boats, tools, diseases, and genetic indicators of all varieties, are among the markers and proxies that leave complexes of interweaving trails and clues that are integral to stories of understanding human movement and knowledge assemblage around the world. The problem is the markers and trails do not all tell the same story. A further complication is that movements, assemblages, and interactions are constrained or enabled in a performative process of coproduction, by genes, by terrain, by climate and sea level changes, by kinship relations, by material technologies, by social and cognitive technologies, knowledge strategies and transmission.

Against this background of multiplicity and coproduction this paper advances four claims. Movement itself often goes unexamined in accounts of human change and development. Understanding human movement requires the inclusion of social and cognitive dimensions in the usual suite of genetic, archaeological, and linguistic dynamics. Highlighting the role of movement in the ways we have come to know the world destabilises the dominant narrative of the journey out of Africa culminating in the sedentary civilization of Western Europe and instead brings to the fore the last two great feats of human exploration—the Polynesian occupation of the Pacific and the Eskimo occupation of the Arctic. Not only were the Polynesians and the Eskimos, unlike most of the human groups who left Africa, making real voyages of discovery, moving into literally unknown and unoccupied regions, they also developed socio-technical complexes enabling them to move in extremely difficult environments that are still central to their cultural identities today. Finally, the multiplicity of stories and the totality of interacting components can, on the one hand, be conceived dynamically as a complex adaptive system in action, or, on the other hand, as being unifiable in a grand synthesis; this paper argues for holding these two approaches in tension with one another.

The stories we tell ourselves about the origins of modernity and civilization, about how humans got to be everywhere, have undergone a profound transformation courtesy of the "geneticization" of history. The dominant narrative of how we left Africa, spread through Asia, Europe, the Americas, and ultimately the Pacific and the Arctic is now being retold in terms of our genes. In many ways this has been a beneficial corrective to a story that previously had been almost entirely Eurocentric, devoted to showing how modernity and civilization were unique and radical, Western, developments arising in the Upper Palaeolithic Revolution around forty to ten thousand years ago. It was in Europe, on this account, that humans first learnt to "paint, carve, dress, weave and exchange goods."[3] They went on to another revolution—the Neolithic, after which they settled down, became sedentary, developed agriculture, built cities, invented writing and the rule of law, and voilá—civilization. In this Eurocentric version of history "the European Upper Palaeolithic became the model for what it means to be human."[4] However, such stories of revolutions are framing devices serving to privilege Europe as the locus of civilization and obscuring the complex set of transformations conducing to modern human behavior that have been in continuous process since at least 200,000 years ago, and possibly even 900,000 years ago. As Bruno Latour puts it, *We Have Never Been Modern*. We have always been becoming modern in the ways we shape our environment as we move through it, and are in turn shaped by it. Hence there are no great divides between humans and nature, or between us and our ancestors.[5]

The gene story, in alliance with recent archaeology, not only claims an African origin for humanity—"we are all Afri-

3
Stephen Oppenheimer, *Out of Eden: The Peopling of the World* (London, 2004), p. 89.

4
Sally McBrearty, "Down with the Revolution," in *Rethinking the Human Revolution: New Behavioural and Biological Perspectives on the Origin and Dispersal of Modern Humans*, ed. Paul Mellars et al. (Cambridge, 2007), pp. 133–151.

5
Bruno Latour, *We Have Never Been Modern* (Cambridge, 1997).

6
Spencer Wells, *Journey of Man: A Genetic Odyssey* (Princeton, 2003).

cans now,"[6] but even more radically, it decenters the origins of modernity, relocating it to Africa. However, this rethinking of the origins of civilization still conceals a number of preconceptions, false perceptions, and misunderstandings that amount to a fundamental *méconnaissance,* as Pierre Bourdieu calls it.

The problem is not just with the over-geneticization of history. There are a number of intersecting misconceptions in the *méconnaissance* that underpins the "greatest story ever told." In telling this story of how humans, i.e., *Homo sapiens sapiens* got to occupy every environmental niche with the exception of Antarctica, it is seldom emphasized that other groups of *Homo sapiens,* our cousins if you like, managed to occupy a good proportion of Africa, Asia, and Europe, though not the Americas, the Pacific, or the northern latitudes. These close relatives, *Homo neanderthalensis* and *Homo erectus* for example, were very nearly as mobile and adaptive as we are. Only recently have we come to acknowledge them as having very similar abilities to our own. They had imaginative self-awareness, as shown by their capacities for symbolization through the use of ochre, making beads, stringing them as necklaces, singing, innovative tool-making, and burying their dead. They quite possibly developed language, given they had a hyoid bone, the essential piece of voice-making apparatus that primates lack. They had the basic prerequisites for mobility—the technologies of connection—string and stories, and they put them into use up to a million years before we did. Indeed their primate predecessors also left from Africa unconstrained by what we see as continental boundaries, moving as climate and environment permitted. The differences between these varieties of humans seem to have been a matter of degree. Where they became significant may have been in the material and cognitive elaboration of symbolization and the strategic development of long-distance exchange networks.[7] That is, humans became more intimately engaged in the making of meaning and value, in developing a socio/cognitive/technical complex that both enabled, and was dependent on, mobility—the capacity to move over long distances to make connections and gather together materials and resources that had more than utilitarian value.

7
Ben Marwick, "Pleistocene Exchange Networks as Evidence for the Evolution of Language," *Cambridge Archaeological Journal* 13, no. 1 (2003), pp. 67–81.

The telling of the human story is always skewed to make some group and their knowledge-tradition look exceptional and different by comparison with another who will be dismissed as primitive, nomadic, or irrational. The Neanderthals are classically portrayed as beetle-browed, thuggish killers who were easily eliminated by us humans because we were smarter. However, this conception no longer fits with the archaeological story that *Homo sapiens sapiens* moved out of Africa into what is now Israel, but were driven out again by Neanderthals who had the capacity to resist in the environment of the day. Only later were humans able to override them, and even then they

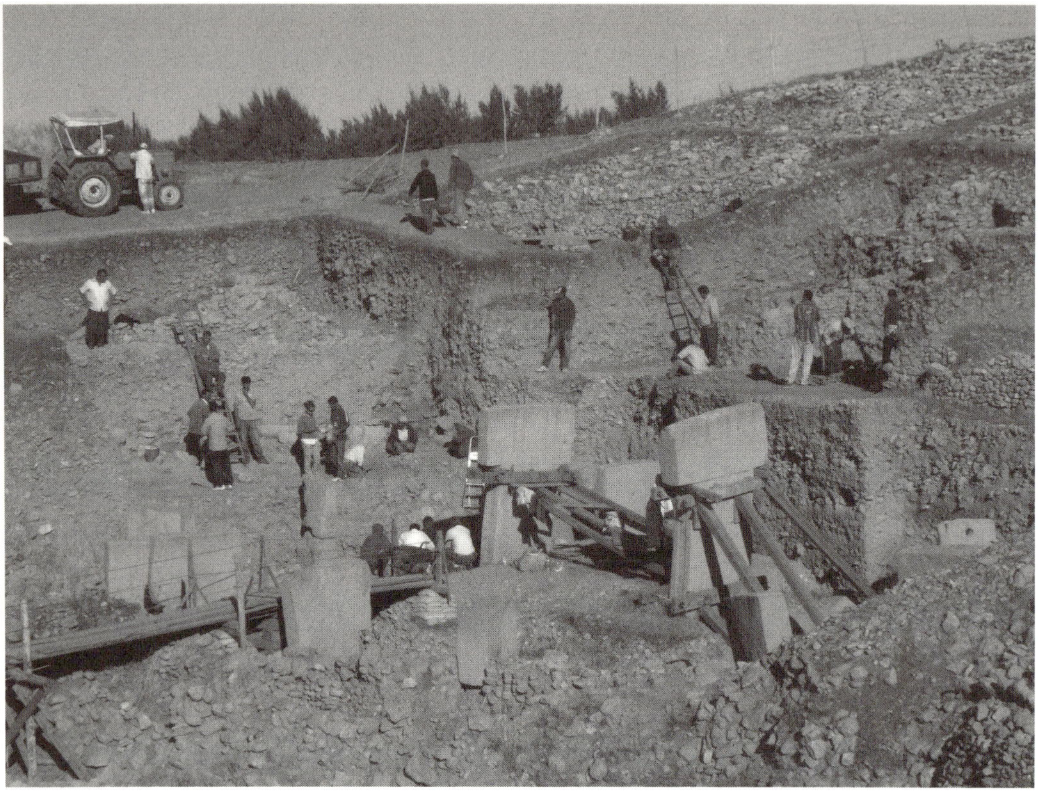

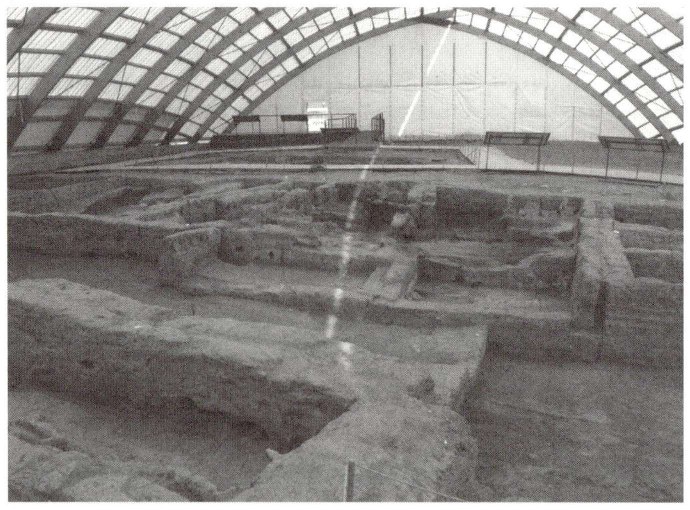

Çatalhöyükk 9.5 thousand-year-old post-agriculture; all domestic spaces, no monumental architecture. Photo: David Turnbull

Gobekli Tepe, 11.5 thousand-year-old preagricultural monumental architecture. Photo: David Turnbull

were cohabiting in some regions for up to 30,000 years before the environment changed to suit *Homo sapiens sapiens* better than it did Neanderthals. And of course, as the winners, we developed both the classificatory terminology and the articulation of its metaphorical usage. The genetic orthodoxy is that modern humans and Neanderthals are unrelated, and this is reinforced by recent archaeological evidence from the south east Pyrenees indicating that Neanderthals occupied the same site, but without any interaction. This story is based on the analysis of a small section of ancient DNA. Full genetic analysis may well reveal that we are all just one variable and interbreeding group, and further archaeological evidence may yet reveal a more complex mosaic of varieties of encounters. The story that could overthrow all previous stories is the discovery of what is claimed to be an entirely new and completely separate species—*Homo floriensis* on the island of Flores in the Indonesian island chain, though I remain skeptical, given the claim is based on only one skull.

My own research concern, as a sociologist of science, is to examine and explain the ways in which we gain knowledge of the world by looking at how knowledge is moved, assembled, and transmitted. One of the reasons for this emphasis on movement is that it tends to be downplayed or even silenced in many accounts of the place of humans in the world and the ways in which the sciences have come to understand it. Fixity in space and place has become the foundation stone of Western rationality and epistemology. In this sedentarist metaphysics, movement is equated with wandering, irrationality, and the primitive, something that needs to be controlled and set in logical, linear order.

The production of scientific knowledge has come to depend on a tightly demarcated organization of space and movement. The emphasis on sedentism, being settled in place, as the touchstone and precondition for civilization and modernity is set against the placeless, nomadic, wandering of indigenes.[8] Again it serves to privilege the "Neolithic revolution" in Europe as the source and origin of all that counts as regularized and legitimate forms of moving and knowing. This space and knowledge story is now destabilized by recent archaeological work at Çatalhöyük and Gobekli Tepe. At Gobekli in eastern Turkey, Klaus Schmidt is excavating a massive mound in which a complex of stone circles was built around 11.5 thousand years ago, with elaborately carved giant T-shaped stones defining the spaces. Gobekli Tepe is so ancient, its builders were hunter-gatherers who had not yet developed agriculture. It consists entirely of public spaces and with no apparent domestic spaces or habitation.[9] By contrast, at Çatalhöyük, Ian Hodder's teams are excavating a large urban agglomeration in central Turkey with a population of up to 10,000 people. Çatalhöyük was built

8
Tim Cresswell, *On The Move: Mobility in the Modern Western World* (New York, 2006); David Turnbull, "Narrative Traditions of Space, Time and Trust in Court: Terra Nullius, 'Wandering' the Yorta Yorta Native Title Claim, and the Hindmarsh Island Bridge Controversy," in *Expertise in Regulation and Law,* ed. Gary Edmond (Aldershot, 2006), pp. 166–183.

9
Klaus Schmidt, "Carved Creatures from the Dawn of Agriculture: Gobekli Tepe, Turkey," in *Discovery: Unearthing the New Treasures of Archaeology,* ed. Brian Fagan (London, 2007), pp. 180–183.

10
Ian Hodder, *The Leopard's Tale: Revealing the Mysteries of Çatalhöyük* (London, 2006).

around 9.5 thousand years ago by people with agriculture, but consists entirely of individual houses—all domestic spaces with no public spaces.[10] These two sites reveal there is no longer any fixed and necessary connection between the way space is ordered and the production of knowledge. People over time have experimented with a variety of ways of assembling, knowing, and moving in the world.

The movement of people into the Pacific ought to be, in theory at least, an ideal model for understanding human migration. It is relatively recent, within the last three to four thousand years, it has clearly defined boundaries and has been largely free of external influences. However, it has proved to be remarkably complex. There is currently no consensus on its origins, its dynamics, or its chronology, reflecting the difficulties that have been encountered by the disciplines involved, including genetics, archaeology, linguistics, anthropology, paleoecology, sociology, history, zoology, botany, history of technology, architecture, mythology, indigenous knowledge, computer simulation, experimental voyaging—the list goes on. The Pacific example shows how hard it is to work backward from a given demographic and linguistic state of affairs: such as the wide geographical spread of the Austronesian languages, and the occupation of the vast expanse of Pacific Ocean islands by Melanesians, Micronesians, and Polynesians. Different researchers have plotted the trails of markers and proxies from genes to pigs and sweet potatoes to canoe design, but again they do not all tell the same story. They point to differing origin points and routes of transmission; a key question is whether or not these stories should be molded into one coherent unified whole.

The relatively recent phase of colonization and terraforming where the Polynesians moved into the remote Pacific, occupying and transforming all the islands including Hawaii, Easter Island, and New Zealand by bringing with them their own plants and animals, has become the subject of a series of debates and controversies. There was a brief period of consensus around the strategic voyaging model, following the early period in which it was claimed that deliberate Pacific voyaging was beyond the capacity of the indigenes and must therefore have been a result of accidental drifting, but that strategic consensus is now being re-evaluated.[11]

11
Geoffrey Irwin, "Voyaging and Settlement," in *Vaka Moana, Voyages of the Ancestors: The Discovery and Settlement of the Pacific*, ed. K. R. Howe (Honolulu, 2009), pp. 54–91.

12
John Cawte Beaglehole, ed., *The Journals of Captain James Cook on His Voyages of Discovery: The Voyage of the Resolution and Discovery 1776–1780*, vol. 1 (Cambridge, 1967), p. cxviii

Captain Cook was the first to recognize that the peoples of the Pacific were of one nation and asked the question that still puzzles us today, "How shall we account for this nation spreading itself so far over this vast ocean?"[12] Cook was of two minds, entertaining the possibility that the one nation of Polynesians had the technical and cognitive capacity to have settled the islands deliberately, while also wondering if some of the islands had been found accidentally. Much of his ambiguity on this issue is reflected in his difficulties in understanding the chart

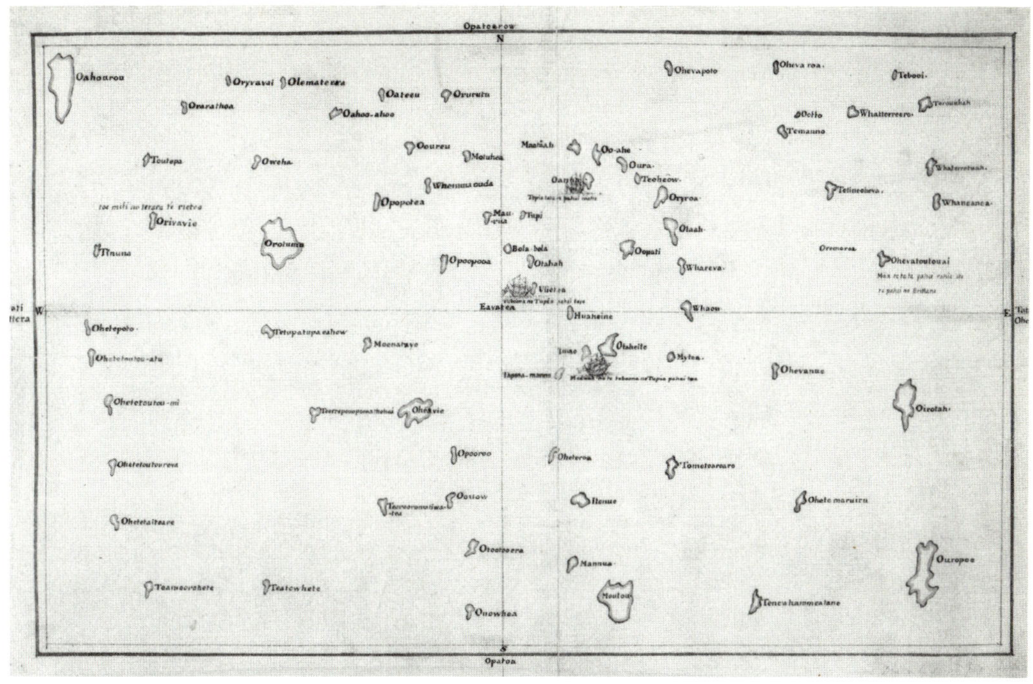

Tupaia's Chart found in Banks's personal collection and preserved in the British Library. Copyright British Library board, all rights reserved (Add. 21593 C)

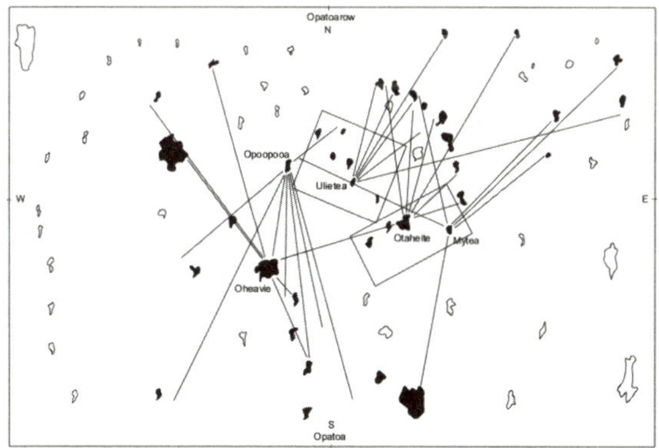

Tupaia's Chart showing the reconstructed plotting diagrams and maps of the Leeward and Windward Society Islands. Anne Di Piazza, and Erik Pearthree. From "A New Reading of Tupaia's Chart," *The Journal of the Polynesian Society* 116, no. 3 (2007), pp. 321–40.

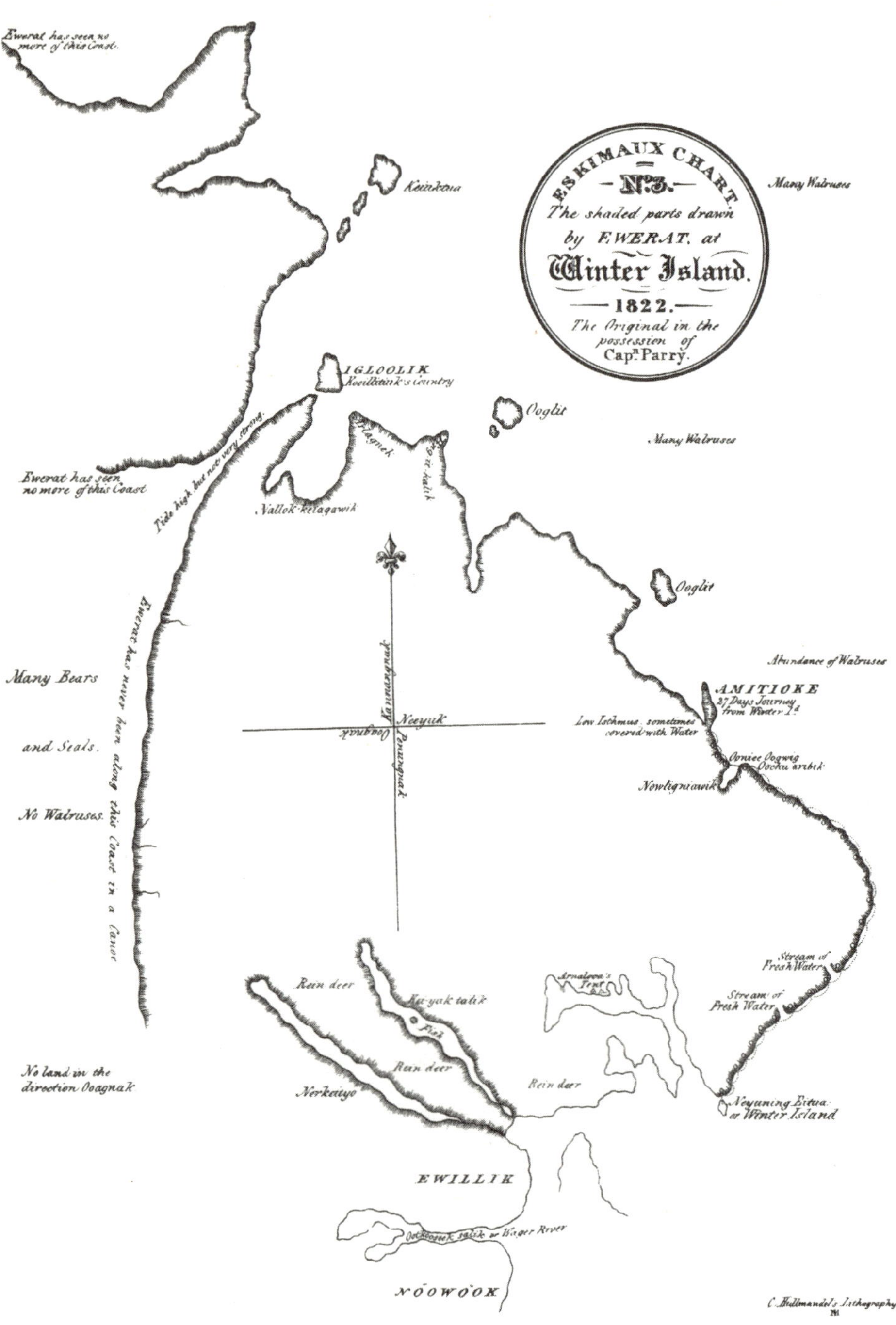

Ewerat's Chart. Ewerat, an Inuit hunter, reveals his knowledge of the navigation and geography of Arctic waters from Aivilik (lower right) to the strait beyond Igloolik (small island, upper left). Source: W. E. Parry, *Second Voyage for the Discovery of a North-West Passage*, 1824

drawn by the Tahitian Tupaia, whom Cook picked up and took with him when he left Tahiti on his first voyage on *Endeavour* in 1769. Tupaia was the leading Pacific navigator of the day and in effect showed Cook around. On the voyage, he drew a chart for Cook of all islands he knew. Tupaia's chart was not only a puzzle for Cook, but for all subsequent analysts. Until recently, it did not appear to make sense, many of the islands seemed to be incorrectly located or were duplicated, leading Cook to have severe reservations about Tupaia's geographical knowledge. Now two French oceanists, in a very telling re-analysis of the chart, have found that "Tupaia's Chart, while having the appearance of a map, is in fact a mosaic of sailing directions or plotting diagrams drawn on paper." They conclude that their unraveling of the Chart

> . . . highlights the difficulties of understanding or sharing knowledge on both sides. Cook, in his own words, believed Tupaia was drawing a map. Tupaia seems indeed to have tried to include distance in his plotting diagrams, thereby going beyond the traditional system of representation. Cook clearly remained fixed in his Cartesian world, adding cardinal points to Tupaia's Chart. But both could look at the manuscript and see their own system represented: Cook reading islands on a grid and Tupaia reading islands radiating out from different centers.[13]

In other words Cook, and Tupaia worked with differing epistemological and ontological assumptions about space and time and how they can be represented, assumptions that were incommensurable and mutually unrecognized. They both thought they were drawing a map, but did not realize they had no common agreement about what maps are or how they record and enable movement. Though they each had an effective system of navigation, they were operating within completely different socio-technical-religious networks. For Cook and his fellow enlightenment European navigators and explorers, the system was one of calculation and long-distance control central to the establishment of empire. For Tupaia and his fellow Polynesian navigators the system was one of exploration and settlement by kin-based replication.[14]

The prevailing orthodox explanation of movement into remote Oceania has been one of deliberate strategic voyaging through the deployment of a complex of socio-technical skills; including canoes capable of windward sailing, a sophisticated body of navigational knowledge, environmental and topographical knowledge, along with social institutions for storing, teaching and reproducing that knowledge. Geoffrey Irwin set the paradigm with computer simulations showing the navigators would have strategically chosen to start off exploring against the wind, thereby ensuring a safe return downwind, leaving to

13
Anne Di Piazza and Erik Pearthree, "A New Reading of Tupaia's Chart," *The Journal of the Polynesian Society* 116, no. 3 (2007), pp. 321–40.

14
Anne Salmond, "Voyaging Exchanges: Tahitian Pilots and European Navigators," in *Canoes of the Grand Ocean*, ed. Anne Di Piazza and Erik Pearthree (Oxford, 2008), pp. 23–46.

15
Geoffrey Irwin, *The Pre-historic Exploration and Colonisation of the Pacific* (Cambridge, 1992).

16
Atholl Anderson et al., "Prehistoric Maritime Migration in the Pacific Islands: An Hypothesis of ENSO Forcing," *The Holocene* 16, no.1 (2006) pp.1–6.

17
John Parkington, *Shore-lines, Strandlopers, and Shell Middens* (Cape Town, 2006)

18
Jon M. Erlandson et al., "The Kelp Highway Hypothesis: Marine Ecol-ogy, the Coastal Migration Theory, and the Peopling of the Americas," *Journal of Island & Coastal Archaeology* 2 (2007), pp. 161–174.

last the most difficult route, sailing downwind to New Zealand with no assurance of return.[15] This paradigm seemed to be confirmed by a multitude of replica voyages. However, Atholl Anderson, a constant critic of this model, argues that the early canoes were very unlikely to have had the windward capacities required. He has recently proposed a model based on seeing the early voyagers as having rather simple canoes, and oppor-tunistically using long-term variability in wind patterns, due to El Nino and the Southern Oscillation (ENSO), to sail eastward and southward across the Pacific.[16] Other models are now proposed based on simulations, evolving canoe design, subsistence strat-egies, etc., opening up the field to a number of widely differing understandings of from where, when, how, with what, and why people moved into and throughout the Pacific.

This pattern of early agreement or dominance of a single model, followed by a proliferation of new research in a variety of disciplines revealing flaws in the early model and provoking calls for a new synthesis that has not yet emerged, has been played out in all the stories of great human movements—out of Africa, into Europe, into Asia, into the Americas and the Arctic. While it is self-evident that the move into the Pacific was by sea, only recently has maritime movement started to challenge the terrestrial orthodoxy as a key component in all the great migrations, but especially out of Africa along the "Great South-ern Arc" and into the Americas. Both are now conceived as a process of "coastal migration" suggesting a mix of strandloping and voyaging.[17]

The story in the case of the Americas is very like that of the Pacific. A dominant paradigm—the "Clovis first model," which holds that settlement of the Americas began after 13,500 years BP—has been overthrown by once controversial but now accepted archaeological dating, and by rethinking the possible entry routes. One of the controversial human occupation sites in question, Monte Verde in Southern Chile, is now largely ac-cepted as dated at circa 14,500 BP, which makes it difficult to accommodate on the "Clovis first" model. This model was based on the assumption that migration into Alaska was only possible across the Beringia land bridge after the Last Glacial Maximum (LGM) at around 13,000 BP, when an ice-free corridor opened up. An alternative coastal route is now plausible, given accu-mulating archaeological evidence of human occupation along the west coast, especially on the islands off California—though such evidence has been hard to obtain because of the rise in sea levels after the LGM. What has really challenged the assumption of terrestrial movement across a land bridge is the articulation of a coastal migration model in which people could have followed the "kelp highway" (the kelp forests of the Pacific rim, which the model suggests were relied on for diet) from Japan to Baja Cali-fornia and thence to Latin and South America.[18] This opens up the possibility of a much earlier time frame and multiple groups overlapping each other and penetrating the interior simultaneously. However, like the Pacific example, there is no agreement on how many migrations there were, what routes they took, and when they occurred. There is broad agreement that the migration or migrations were out of north east Asia and were separated from the migration of the predecessors of the modern Eskimo and Inuit by around 10,000 years, but there is no agreement on dates, numbers of migrations, or routes. There is some evidence that the land bridge may have been flooded as early as 11,000 years ago all of which tends to support a coastal migration route along with other possible overland routes.

Thus it appears that all the great migrations into south east Asia, into the Pacific, and into the Americas may have utilized a coastal path, and that they could only have occurred with the deployment of socio-technical complexes sharing some common broad characteristics. They would also have shared some climate constraints and sea level changes. The forms of movement and interaction would have been entirely dependent on the specific historical context, but bringing the movements into focus requires the recognition of its inherent complexity.

As humans move in a given environment, they are not simply moving through it, they shape and affect it, and vice versa, the environment shapes them. This coevolutionary adaptive process, or coproduction, is historical, time dependent, and hence irreversible. However, the process of movement is much more than an ecological niche construction or a gene/habitat interaction. As the anthropologist Clive Gamble argues "what characterizes social life in humans rather than hominids is our ability to extend social relations across space and time."[19] That extension is basically performative, being based in our bodily movement. It is our bodies that give us our location, our spatial and temporal orientation in the world. In the process of making connections cognitively, socially, and linguistically, we come to know the world and to alter it.[20] We also deploy tools, materials, artifacts, and knowledge in complex systems of trade and exchange, thus proliferating "chains of connection" in social networks.[21] In tracing these chains of connection, in following the trails of languages, genes, canoes, or pigs, we are, at the same time, creating cognitive trails that deploy the ontologies, epistemologies, and methodologies of our own disciplines. The seductive dream in the minds of many researchers is of a grand synthesis, a convergence of all disciplinary data, under one of the many banners that have been variously proposed, including archaeogenetics, phylogeography, genomic anthropology. Such a synthetic consilience is an ideal toward which to aim, but it is one which should be subject to constant challenge. Rather than restricting the possibilities, I would advocate acknowledging that the process of understanding a complex adaptive system like

19
Clive Gamble, *Origins and Revolutions: Human Identity in Earliest Prehistory* (Cambridge, 2007), pp. 8–39.

20
David Turnbull, "Maps, Narratives and Trails: Performativity, Hodology, Distributed Knowledge in Complex Adaptive Systems—An Approach to Emergent Mapping," *Geographical Research* 45, no. 2 (2007), pp. 140–49.

21
Gamble 2007 (see note 47), pp. 212–13; D. J. Mulvaney, "'The Chain of Connection': The Material Evidence," in *Tribes and Boundaries in Australia*, ed. by Nicolas Peterson (Canberra, 1976), pp. 72–95.

human movement can itself be conceived as just such a system.

One of the key components on which all forms of movement depend is a social technology of kinship—a network of relatedness, bonding, and obligations that enables the transmission of property and knowledge across generations through a classification of friends, enemies, and strangers. These conceptions of kinship and relatedness are social and cultural constructs and do not map directly onto genetic and biological relationships. Hence the necessity of finding ways in which the differing stories of relatedness and movement can be enabled to work together.

The development of complex forms of social cognition is, Clive Gamble suggests, a prerequisite for overcoming the limitations of co-presence and extending relationships in space and time. To get to Australia, kinship was needed just as much as boats.[22] A view that is consonant with Robin Dunbar's "social brain hypothesis."[23] Dunbar argues that "Primate societies are implicit social contracts established to solve the ecological problems of survival and reproduction more effectively than they could do on their own. Primate societies work as effectively as they do in this respect because they are based on deep social bonding that is cognitively expensive. Thus it is the computational demands of managing complex interactions that has driven neocortical evolution." In large part the symbolization and feedback essential to the development of such social networks depends on keeping track of relatedness and kinship through forms of telling: performing and representation, story telling, singing, dancing, painting, building, and weaving. It is now apparent that each of the so-called dispersals needs reconceiving, not as simply mass migrations or demic diffusions, but as human movements that were relatively fast and strategic, requiring great flexibility in a diversity of environments, necessitating complex information exchange systems that allow group planning and feedback. Such information exchange systems are typically an integral component of a socio-cognitive-technical complex, in which a wider interacting system of relationships, language, materials, genes, and people, were coproduced in the process of human movement. An especially salient example of the social, cognitive, and material components essential to the strategic approach to moving into an environment never encountered before is that of the Inuit and Eskimos, for whom, in the special conditions of the Arctic, the complex of movement technologies are still fundamental to their way of life today. The extreme climate conditions of the Arctic meant that they had to develop material technologies allowing them to create a series of mobile "survivable microclimates" including string, needles, finely sewn weatherproof clothing, igloos, fire, wolf taming, sledges and boats or canoes, and sophisticated fishing technologies harpoons, hooks, and nets.[24]

22
Clive Gamble, "Kinship and Material Culture: Archaeological Implications of the Human Diaspora," in *Early Human Kinship: From Sex to Social Reproduction*, ed. Nicolas Allen et al. (Oxford, 2008), pp. 27–40.

23
Robin Dunbar, "The Social Brain and the Cultural Explosion of the Human Revolution," in *Rethinking the Human Revolution* 2007 (see note 4), pp. 91–98.

24
Richard A. Rogers et al., "How the Door Opened: The Peopling of the New World," *Human Biology* 64, no. 3 (1992) pp. 281–302.
David Turnbull, "String and Stories," in *Encyclopedia of the History of Science, Technology and Medicine in Non-western Cultures*, ed. H. Selin (Berlin, 2008).

25
Claudio Aporta, "The Trail as Home: Inuit and Their Pan-Arctic Network of Routes," *Human Ecology* 37 (2009), pp. 131–146

But in addition to these material technologies, as Claudio Aporta has shown, the Inuit had to solve their specific local problems of "passing on information about territory from season to season and generation to generation" created by the reality that "they can only travel in the Arctic in the winter after the snow creates a new blank territory." To do this they deploy an Inuit socio-cognitive technology of knowledge communication and exchange in the form of a "network of lived story trails"; a form of knowledge movement and assemblage that, like Tupaia's, is unrecognized in the wider society, but which in this case has often proved superior to GPS based navigation.[25]

Aporta reveals the geographic extent of the Inuit's sophisticated network of routes, the way the Inuit have made use of an intimate knowledge of the Arctic environment, and how their trails represent significant channels of communication and exchange across the territory.

To the Inuit, the Arctic is a network of trails, connecting communities to their distant neighbors and to fishing lakes and hunting grounds in between. What is remarkable is that although the trails are not permanent features of the landscape, their locations are remembered and transmitted orally and through the experience of travel. They do not use maps to travel or to represent geographic information. Rather, the journey along the trail, or the story of the journey, becomes one of the main instruments for transmitting the information.

The memory of the trail is intertwined with individual and collective memories of previous trips, as well as with relevant environmental information—the conditions of the snow and ice, the shape of snowdrifts, the direction of winds—and place names in the Inuktitut language. The trails are not permanent, but disappear when the sled tracks get covered after a blizzard and as the snow and ice melt at the end of each spring. Nevertheless, the spatial itinerary remains in people's memory and comes to life again when individuals make the next trip. The trails are "lived" rather than simply traveled.[26]

26
"Inuit Trails Represent Complex Social Network Spanning Canadian Arctic," *ScienceDaily*, February 15, 2009

This movement-based framework provides a profoundly different epistemology and sense of identity. As Tim Ingold puts it, "For the Inuit, as soon as a person moves he becomes a line. To hunt for an animal, or to find another human being who may be lost, you lay one line of tracks through the expanse, looking for signs of another line that may lead you to your quarry. Thus the entire country is perceived as a network of lines rather than a continuous surface."[27] Claudio Aporta sums it up: "travelling [for the Inuit] was not a transitional activity between one place and another, but a way of being . . . the act of travelling from or to a particular location plays a part in defining who the traveller is."[28]

27
Tim Ingold, *Lines: A Brief History*. (London, 2007) p. 76

28
Claudio Aporta, "Routes, Trails and Tracks: Trail Breaking among the Inuit of Igloolik," *Études/Inuit/Studies* 28, no. 2 (2004), pp. 9–38, here p. 13

Human movement from a performative/emergent perspective is a continuously evolving complex adaptive system with multiple interacting and transforming components, including genes, environments, language, cognition, material, and social technologies, constrained by the conditions for possibility, such as climate and sea levels.

What then does this conception of the movement of humans through the environment do for ways in which to think about how to follow the trails of genes, proxies, and markers, trails which are themselves coproducing a diversity of cognitive environments? How should the reflexive process of understanding how we came to be the way we are as a species be conceived? As I indicated earlier there is an ongoing attempt at synthesis and consilience which has a powerful and important dynamic, in which geneticists, linguists, and archaeologists, etc., are constantly looking at each other's data and models for clues on origins, dating, and connections. However, while such a dynamic consilience is laudable as goal-directed research, it is less desirable if it moves toward an insistence on commensurability between disciplines or towards subordination to the norms of one discipline. What I would suggest is that three things need to be kept clearly in mind. First, because it is in the nature of science that all disciplines are subject to radical evaluation of their ontological assumptions and models on an irregular basis, it is vital that such assumptions and models be challenged with alternative conceptions. Second, the suggested performative conception of human movement as a complex adaptive system ought to be reflected in the ways the disciplines involved interact. Finally what needs to be included in all this are indigenous perspectives. Much research in the area has the implication of telling people "who they really are," where they come from, who they are related to, and what counts as authoritative knowledge. Such matters of identity, relationship, and authority are central to every cultural group's conception of themselves and are intensely political. The people who are directly affected must also have a voice in the process.

Tom Dillehay, the archaeologist renowned for his excavation of the Monte Verde site in Chile, has had to meet the most damning of criticisms over many years, from the "Clovis first" establishment. They simply insisted that his dating must be wrong because it could unquestioningly be assumed there could only have been an entry route over the Beringia land bridge after the Last Glacial Maximum (LGM). Now that Dillehay's empirical work has eventually been accepted, he has written a very important reflective piece on how to proceed in understanding the peopling the Americas, which could be extended to all understandings of human movement and historical change generally.

He argues that the question of how people populated the Americas must be answered at all scales and by all disciplines. Along these lines, researchers need to anticipate the first peopling process empirically and theoretically, observe its material, skeletal, and molecular correlates, and its variation and linkage at different scales, and relate them to similar issues on a global scale, meaning cross-cultural comparison to the study of early migration behavior in Old World archaeology, as well. Variability in the peopling process can be studied by a wide range of paradigms, including biological, ecological, and anthropological paradigms. Flexibility between local, hemispherical, and global questions, between context and artifact, between essentialism and materialism, between reductionism and emergence, and between different datasets to create inclusive analyses and more theoretical understanding of the process in an interdisciplinary manner is one goal. Another is to integrate the sheer complexity of multiple databases beyond the traditional focal points of sites, artifacts, genes, and skeletons and integrate them into a descriptive and analytical whole. To do so requires both an interdisciplinary scientific and theoretical framework.[29]

Such an integrated process cannot be one of synthesis and commensurability alone: it must allow the productive tension of working with and against an emergent, nonlinear process of interactive multiplicity and incommensurability. We need to imagine a space in which all our storied trails can be performed together, where mobility and connection can flourish.

29
Tom D. Dillehay, "Probing Deeper into First American Studies," *PNAS* 106, no. 4 (2009), pp. 971–78.

Arctic Geopolitics & Autonomy

Post–Cold War Arctic Geopolitics: Where Are the Peoples and the Environment?

Lassi Heininen

In the early twenty-first century there are two main discourses on geopolitics and security of the Arctic or the High North (the term used in Canada and Scandinavia for the Arctic waters and rimlands). They offer contrasting accounts of the High North as it has emerged in the post–cold war period. The mainstream discourse emphasizes its stability and peacefulness and the absence of armed conflicts or likelihood of them.[1] In this account the industrialized and militarized High North of the cold war started to thaw in the late nineteen-eighties and was transformed from a situation of confrontation to one of international cooperation. This produced increased interrelations between people(s) and civil societies, as well as transboundary cooperation between states. The other discourse, a minority view, argues that the Arctic, framed narrowly as the waters of the Arctic Ocean, has the potential to become a "race" for natural resources, particularly those related to energy like oil and natural gas, and consequently, to escalate in the direction of armed conflict.[2]

There are geopolitical and economic realities corresponding to real changes in the Arctic.

The resource-rich region is under pressure for an increasing utilization of its energy resources, as it has been over the centuries for fish stocks and marine mammals. Its northern seas are the subject of maritime border disputes, particularly the boundaries between exclusive economic zones (EEZ) demarcating the continental shelves of the littoral states. Efforts by Canada and Russia to safeguard the sovereignty and control of actual and potential shipping lanes in their northern waters have attracted international attention. Furthermore, the land claims of Arctic indigenous peoples are linked to debates and conflicts over ownership, access, and use of land, water, and sea ice. These are the parameters around which the discourses of northern geopolitics are discussed: those of conflict and cooperation.

The predicted conflicts have not (yet) materialized. The Arctic region is stable and peaceful. There is increasing circumpolar cooperation among indigenous peoples' organizations. There is renewed region-building with states as major actors. There is emerging a new kind of relationship between the region and the outside world.[3] That much is clear. However, there are two other perspectives that deserve more attention and can enable us to approach Arctic geopolitics that go beyond the familiar terms of conflict and cooperation. First, there is a new and significant multi-dimensional geopolitical, geo-economic and environmental change that has occurred in the High North. Second, the region is playing a changing and more important role in world politics. These two closely related perspectives, when combined, raise a key question that has been consistently overlooked in the cold war legacy of Arctic geopolitical studies.

1

See Lassi Heininen, "Circumpolar International Relations and Cooperation," Lassi Heininen and Chris Southcott, eds., *Globalization and the Circumpolar North* (Fairbanks, 2010), pp. 265–304.

2

See Scott G. Borgerson, "Arctic Meltdown: The Economic and Security Implications of Global Warming," *Foreign Affairs* (March/April 2008); Brian Beary, "Race for the Arctic: Who Owns the Region's Undiscovered Oil and Gas?" *Global Researcher: Exploring International Perspectives* 2, no. 8 (August 2008), pp. 213–42. <www.GLOBALRESEARCHER.COM>

3

As pointed out in the *Arctic Human Development Report* (Akureyri, 2004).

Where, in the geopolitical analysis, are the peoples of the Arctic and their relationship to its environment? In the second part of this essay, I focus on the role of northern indigenous peoples as international actors, and the importance of their environmental "awakening."

A Spectrum of Changing Visions

Classical geopolitics privileges the point of view of states. This projects the Arctic primarily as a reserve of natural resources and a space for the military. This does not, however, paint a faithful picture of the Arctic, since it has been framed by a spectrum of visions—ranging from an external image as a frozen colonial periphery, to an internal image as a homeland of people(s) confronting many changes within the region, including geopolitical issues.

One aim of this cahier is to take a longer view of the Arctic, recognizing that its history is crucial to understanding its character. David Turnbull discusses in his essay how relations between peoples within and across the region, and between them and the peoples of lower latitudes, took shape some thousands of years ago, involving complex assemblages of strategies, knowledge, and technologies. This very spatial human history developed long before any state entered the High North. Early communication, networks, and crossroads of northern indigenous cultures included frequent traveling, exchanges of goods and experiences, trade, marriages, migration, and reciprocal visits within the circumpolar north.[4] Seen in the context of this timeframe, colonization and militarization are, indeed, fairly recent phenomena. The Viking Age saw the emergence of networks of communication between the North Atlantic, northern Europe, and Russia along east–west as well as north–south trade routes.[5] Centuries later, European explorers ventured into northern seas to search for new wealth and a new sea route to China and India. They were followed by thousands of whalers. Indigenous and other local peoples established long-lasting contacts with traders (including some whalers), and were followed by fur traders and missionaries.[6]

The advance of states in the North happened incrementally, step-by-step, over centuries. They took control of land and water by establishing a host of regulations: giving hunting privileges in northern "no-man's" forests, trading with northern peoples and controlling the terms of trade, collecting taxes, building churches, establishing garrisons, utilizing natural resources, occupying lands and waters, and finally legitimizing all this by drawing national borders. Thus, colonialism was not an abstract political force; it brought explorers, missionaries, tax collectors, newcomers/settlers, and state authorities. These groups were armed with definitions and "geo-names," such as

4
Peter Schweitzer, "Traveling Between Continents," *Arctic Research of the United States* 11 (Spring/Summer 1997), p. 68; Andre Golovnev, "Two Northern Stories Meet Two Northern Projects," *North Meets North: Proceedings of the First Northern Research Forum*, ed. T. S. Björnsson et al. (Akureyri, 2001), pp. 45–48.

5
Lassi Heininen, "Different Images of the Arctic, and the Circumpolar North in World Politics," *Knowledge and Power in the Arctic: Conference Proceedings*, Paula Kankaanpää, Sanna Ovaskainen, Leo Pekkala & Monica Tennberg, eds. (Rovaniemi, 2007), pp. 124–34.

6
Francis Abele and Thierry Rodon, "Inuit Diplomacy in the Global Era: The Strengths of Multilateral Internationalism," *Canadian Foreign Policy* 13, no. 3 (2007), pp. 45–63; Chris Southcott, "History of Globalization in the Circumpolar North," in Heininen and Southcott 2010 (see note 1), pp. 23–55.

7
See Ken Coates, "The Discovery of the North: Towards a Conceptual Framework for the Study of Northern / Remote Regions," *The Northern Review*, no. 12/13 (Summer 1994/Winter 1994).

8
Immanuel Wallerstein, "Development: Lodestar or Illusion?" A talk at the Distinguished Speaker series, Center for Advanced Study of International Development, Michigan State University (October 22, 1987), pp. 7–8; also Heikki Kerkelä, *Vanhan maailman peilissa: Modernin yhteiskunnan synty ja pohjoinen aineistoa* (Tampere, 1996).

the label "Arctic" that we take for granted—tools to describe and control these "unmapped" regions for political purposes.[7] As a result, there is a multiplicity of different images—internal and external—some existing in competition, while others are shared by the peoples living in the North, scholars working on northern issues, or enthusiasts of the North.

The capitalist world-economy is the background context against which the advance of states needs to be framed. The socioeconomic development of the northern regions, notably from a hunting-herding-gathering economy into industrialization has happened in a short time period with frontier capitalism advancing unevenly at different speeds in different parts of the Arctic, but following a clear pattern. Immanuel Wallerstein famously described the relationship between core and periphery in terms of "the accumulation of capital, the social organization of local production processes, and the political organization of the state structures in creation."[8] This invites us to consider more carefully relationships extending to other regions and communities while not forgetting the importance of the unified state system with its pronounced emphasis on national interests and territorial sovereignty. The power of economic and political elites, and nationalistic and militaristic interests should not be overlooked. One of the key impacts of states has been to transform borders, once permeable or negotiable, into fixed boundaries that can be patrolled or closed. This runs against the spirit of the tradition of a "borderless" space viewed either as a frontier for fruitful communication or as a borderland for exchange of goods and ideas. No wonder that the cold war period did so much to freeze interregional and international cooperation within the region.

First Geopolitical Change

Northerners in the nineteen-eighties began to consider the Arctic's potential as a means of re-establishing horizontal connections and functional cooperation across the cold war political divide. Inspired by the international movement of indigenous peoples, the Saami and the Inuit had begun nation-building projects in part to fulfill a desire to recognize and interpret the circumpolar North as a region in its own right. They began defining themselves across borders as one nation and organizing their joint political bodies such as the Saami Council and the Inuit Circumpolar Council (ICC).

Severe environmental neglect and damage was one of the lasting legacies of the cold war. Radioactive leaks and waste, together with other toxic industrial and military substances, have in recent decades become concentrated in northern regions. This was exacerbated by long-range air and water pollution concentrated by atmospheric winds in the Arctic and absorbed in still higher concentrations up the food chain. Northern peoples became acutely concerned with the declining state of their ecosystems, and responded by becoming much more active in environmental cooperation. International environmental organizations, such as Greenpeace International and the World Wildlife Fund, also initiated their own programs and campaigns for Arctic environmental protection. The growing recognition of the threats posed by anthropogenic climate change pushed environmental issues into the foreground for northern residents all around the Arctic, encouraging them to examine the threats to their traditional livelihoods and cultures, as well as the resilience of core activities such as fishing and catching marine mammals.

This new situation of a growing, "wild" international cooperation, or "connectivity," between non-state actors pushed the governments of the Arctic states to pay attention to issues related to the fragile Arctic environment. Bilateral agreements on scientific and environmental cooperation were signed as environmental protection became a new field of foreign policy. The so-called Murmansk speech by the Soviet President Mikhail Gorbachev gave the initial impetus for the current intergovernmental cooperation in the Arctic.[9] The Arctic Environmental Protection Strategy in 1991[10] and a plethora of other post-cold war initiatives established new institutions of international cooperation, such as the Arctic Council in 1996.

Consequently, the Arctic geopolitics ceded ground to more human-oriented concerns,[11] and the new international cooperation of the nineteen-nineties was a significant and fundamental structural change in circumpolar geopolitics and international relations. This emphasized the importance of cooperation across national borders with a view to fostering common and comprehensive security and promoting a new kind of human development and democracy that aimed to include indigenous and regional voices and space for their different aspirations for self-determination and autonomy.[12]

Today the political landscape of the Arctic can be interpreted as a success story in the post–cold war era. The central aim of the main new intergovernmental and non-governmental organizations, forums, and networks—to decrease military tension and increase political stability and peace—has been fulfilled. Further, we can define the state of circumpolar geopolitics and international relations in terms of three levels or scales: first, increasing circumpolar cooperation and intentional mobilization by indigenous peoples' organizations and subnational governments; second, region-building with states as major actors; and third, a new kind of relationship between the circumpolar North and the outside world.[13] Taken together, these three factors arguably portray a much more complex, multilayered role for the Arctic in world politics than in former colonial days. But what are the prospects that this might change?

9
Mikhail Gorbachev, "The Speech of President Mihail Gorbachev on October 2, in Murmansk," *Pravda*, October 2, 1987.

10
"Rovaniemi Declaration," signed by the Eight Arctic Nations, June 14, 1991 Rovaniemi, Finland.

11
Sanjay Chaturvedi, "Arctic Geopolitics: Then and Now," in *The Arctic: Environment, People, Policy*, ed. Mark Nuttall and T.V. Callaghan (Amsterdam, 2000).

12
Willy Östreng, ed., *National Security and International Environmental Cooperation in the Arctic—The Case of the Northern Sea Route* (Dordrecht, 1999), pp. 16–17.

13
Lassi Heininen, "Circumpolar International Relations and Geopolitics," in *Arctic Human Development Report* (Akureyri, 2004).

Another Geopolitical Change

The "soft" power represented by the rich variety of multilateral actors has innovative and flexible structures, but are they strong enough to count where there are issues of sovereignty and national security, and where the hegemony of power based on realist thinking remains central to the thinking and control of agendas by key states? With the growing global strategic importance of the Arctic, it is certainly possible to argue that the post–cold war period in the Arctic is over, notwithstanding the presence of its soft power institutions.[14] So which case is more plausible?

Let's not forget that the Arctic is no *terra nullius.* Its territories are under national sovereignty with fixed national borders; even most maritime boundaries have been agreed upon. Furthermore, the entire region enjoys considerable lively cooperation between states, with the Arctic Council being the most important soft-law instrument.[15] Arctic states are still the major actors of the region and are a crucial source of regional political and social stability through intergovernmental cooperation, through channels that do not significantly impinge on national sovereignty or strategic interests.

Admittedly, climate change with its severe impacts precipitating physical change, such as the increasing melting of sea ice or the collapse of areas of permafrost, brings home the growing level of uncertainty that contributes to the vulnerability of this region.[16] Passage through the Arctic, particularly Russia's Northern Sea Route, is now more accessible than was once the case. This mobilizes a range of international interests that are positioning themselves in new ways around navigation and environmental issues. This state change in the sea ice in particular, and the climate more generally, will test the resilience of the fragile Arctic ecosystems. The severe socioeconomic impacts of climate change endanger both environmental and human security as well as pose questions about the state sovereignty of Canada and Russia.

The position of the eight Arctic states is changing, nevertheless. More strategic emphasis is now placed on sovereignty and national interests linked to climate change or energy security. Evidence is that the littoral states are using all legal rights available to them in the United Nations Convention on the Law of the Sea (UNCLOS) to establish Exclusive Economic Zones or to make submissions for sovereign rights to resources on the main basin of the Arctic Ocean. All of the Arctic states (except Sweden) have recently approved their own strategy or policy on Arctic or northern issues, setting out their national priorities.

This new position is best illustrated by the two ministerial meetings of the five Arctic Ocean littoral states that took place in May 2008 and in March 2010.[17] The three nations without

14
Lassi Heininen, "Pohjoiset alueet muutoksessa – geopoliittinen näkökulma," *Politiikka* 1 (2010).

15
See Timo Koivurova, "Limits and Possibilities of the Arctic Council in a Rapidly Changing Scene of Arctic Governance," *Polar Record,* online article (accessed September 9, 2009).

16
See Nils Peter Gleditsch, "The Liberal Moment Fifteen Years On," *International Studies Quarterly* 52, no. 4 (December 2008).

17
See "Ilulissat Declaration: Arctic Ocean Conference in Ilulissat, Greenland, 27–29 May 2008," *Arctic Idea* (August 2008).

High Arctic coastlines and continental shelves (Sweden, Finland, Iceland) as well as the six Permanent Participants (i.e., Indigenous Peoples' organizations) took exception to being excluded from such important discussions, leading commentators more generally to ask whether this might jeopardize or marginalize the Arctic Council itself. The counterargument is that because the Arctic Council is a soft-law instrument, it has avoided issues dealing with industrial-scale exploitation of natural resources (oil, natural gas, and marine mammals) and traditional security. Whether this signals a return to the politics of a more lasting and strident nationalism is unclear.

Without doubt the geostrategic importance of the Arctic in world politics and the globalized world economy is increasing. Besides the region's continuing military-strategic importance to the major nuclear powers, the growing interest in its rich energy resources and associated financial instruments, together with the growing potential value of trans-Arctic sea routes has put the Arctic squarely on the world map. Powers from outside the region—in Asia (China, Japan, and South Korea) and Europe (France, the United Kingdom and the European Union)—are now actively exploring their policy options for the Arctic. More importantly, the United Nations has an important role to play through the Intergovernmental Panel on Climate Change (IPCC) and the above-mentioned UNCLOS.

Beyond the geostrategic interests, knowledge practices and their implicit values also politicize the Arctic on the global stage.[18] The reputation of the region as a scientific "laboratory" or "workshop for research" amplifies the attention given to its environment and climate change. This is accompanied by a growing realization that the Arctic's ecosystems make a major contribution to the diversity of nature on Earth—the old idea of the Arctic as a barren region is wrong and now discredited. This new epistemological attention to the Arctic as a sentinel region for the globe is reflected in some measure in innovations in political and legal arrangements, as for example patents and new intellectual property rights. Discussions about reforms to principles of governance invite public debate. This may help to explain why the Arctic is now to offer new fertile scope for interventions and explorations in contemporary art, such as the arts-science interactions represented by the Arctic Perspective Initiative. Peripheral spaces usually offer more room for brainstorming, innovation, and the exploration of human-nature relationships than the core centers.[19]

The official discourse of northern cooperation and conflict carries the burden of realist/classical geopolitical theory and its fixation with mystifying national security and attending to state sovereignty and nationalistic interests. Instead I now want to explore how indigenous peoples as international actors pursue their own agendas for northern cooperation. For them the

18
Lassi Heininen, "Impacts of Globalization, and the Circumpolar North in World Politics," *Polar Geography* 29, no. 2 (2005).

19
As, for example, the Arctic Human Development Report (Akureyri, 2004) has pointed out in its major findings.

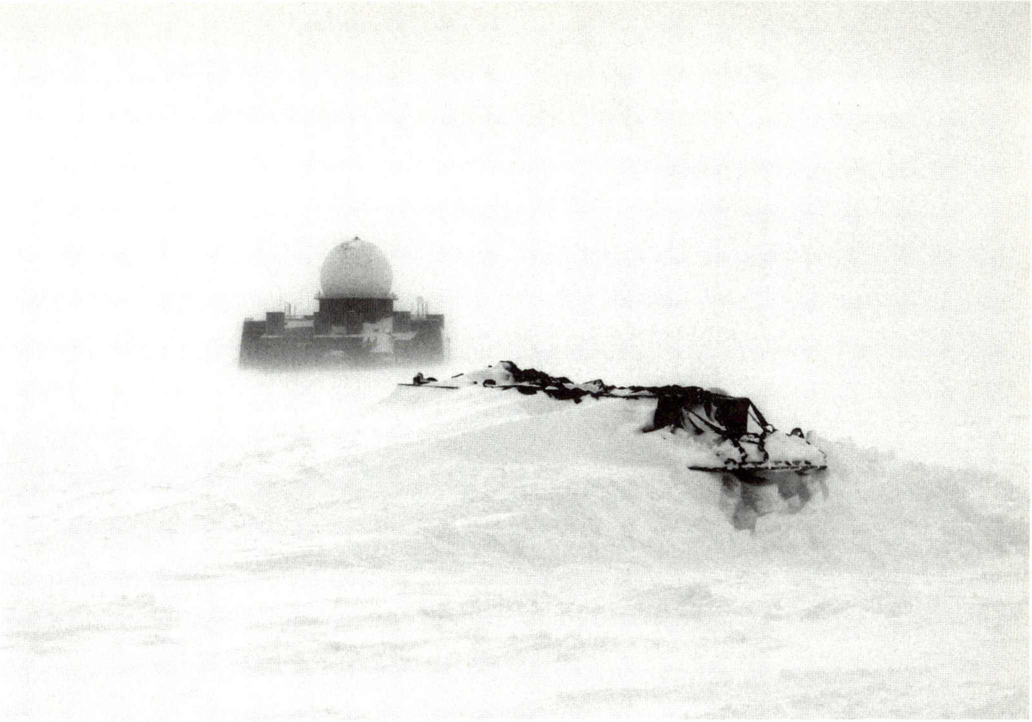

Abandoned Early Warning Radar Site, part of the former DEW (Distant Early Warning) system, Kangerlussuaq, Greenland. Photo: Catherine Crouch, USAF/DefenseImagery.mil

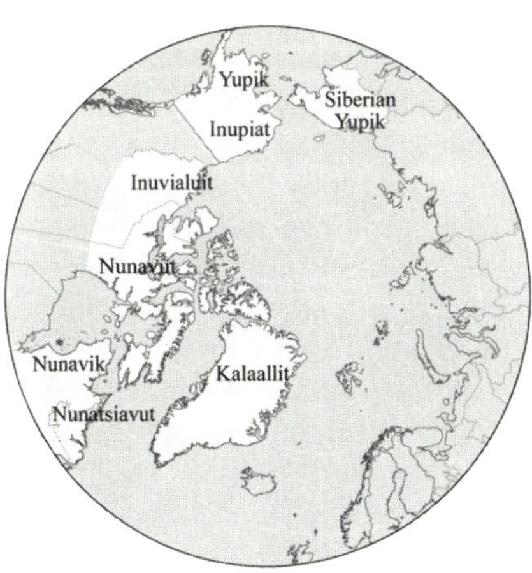

Map showing the members of the Inuit Circumpolar Conference.
Author: Kmusser/Wikimedia Commons

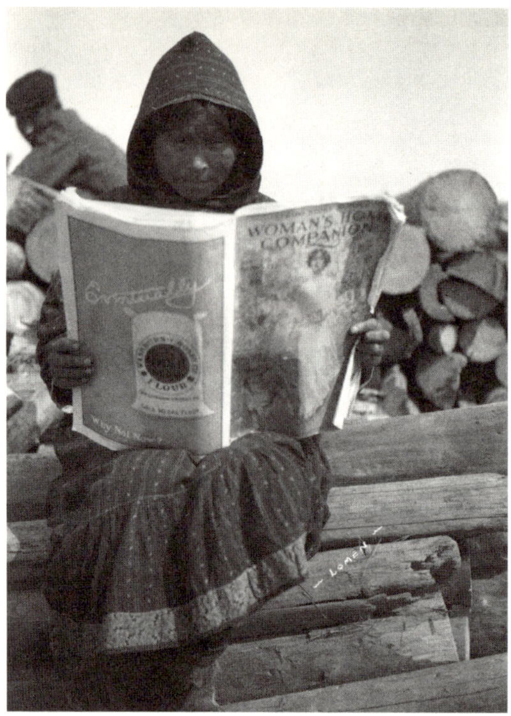

Inuit woman reading *Woman's Home Companion* magazine, Alaska. ca. 1903–1915.
Photo: Lomen Brothers, Nome, Alaska. Glenbow Museum

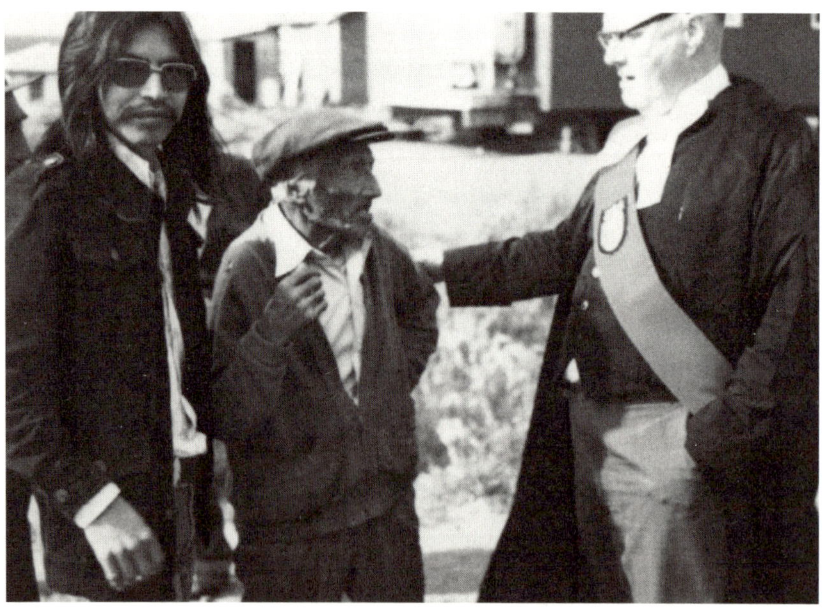

Judge William Morrow at land claims hearings, Fort Norman, Northwest Territories.
Summer 1973. Left to right: James Wah-Shee, president of N. W. T. Indian Brotherhood;
Julian (surname not known), aged 90 years; Judge William Morrow. Glenbow Museum.

20
Yrjö Haila, "Johdanto: Mikä ympäristö?" in Y. Haila and P. Jokinen, eds. *Ympäristöpolitiikka: Mikä ympäristö, kenen politiikka* (Jyväskylä, 2001), p. 9.

21
For more about the Saami, see Kristiina Karppi & Johan Eriksson, eds., "Conflict and Cooperation in the North," *Kulturens Frontlinjer, Skrifter från forskningsprogrammet KULTURGRÄNS NORR* 38 (Umeå, 2002).

22
Natalia Loukacheva, *The Arctic Promise: Legal and Political Autonomy of Greenland and Nunavut* (Toronto, 2007), pp. 30–32.

23
Abele and Rodon 2007 (see note 6), pp. 45–63.

environment is nothing less than "the material basis for human existence," and is in danger of being "destroyed as a result of human activities,"[20] particularly for the peoples living in the Arctic!

Indigenous Peoples as International Actors

From the perspective of international law, the Arctic is divided into the eight Arctic states by national borders and the territories and internal waters fall under their national sovereignty. This state-centric viewpoint does not however represent the whole picture. The Arctic region is home to many different indigenous peoples, including the Inuit in North America, the Nenets in Russia, and the Saami in Fennoscandia. These peoples have become effective actors with a considerable voice both in their domestic and in international affairs, where institutionalized northern cooperation is a key component.[21]

Greenland is a particularly interesting case study because the Inuit there make up almost ninety percent of the population. Greenland negotiated with Denmark a legal subnational government, which then acquired responsibility and greater autonomy in several policy areas, including language policy and the utilization of natural resources.[22] Greenland has since assumed self-determination through a 2009 referendum, a significant step toward full independence. That said, Greenland is legally still under Danish rule, including control of foreign affairs and defence.

Running through this book is the idea that autonomy finds political expression in different forms and practices. Both the meaning and usage of the term *nation* have long been contested. Early modern usage referred to ethnic groups or peoples as nations, whereas it was subsequently appropriated by nation-states. Most northern indigenous peoples have since been minorities in their nation-states, and consequently, their main aim is to find opportunities to secure the right to self-determination. To that end many indigenous groups today describe themselves as nations within nations (or across nations), and are prying open the assumption that nationhood must be synonymous with discrete territorial boundaries. These definitional and semantic shifts fit with the global trend to redefine and treat indigenous peoples as international actors—nations with a population, an identity, a right to self-determination, and, it is hoped, a territory in the future. Crucially for this book, these meanings can retain considerable continuity with the traditional grassroots networks of communications, witnessed by oral histories, written records, and institution-building from precolonial times through to the present.[23]

Take for example, the Saami people, whose homeland is divided by the national borders of four states. Mentally there has been a strong feeling of possessing the unity of one nation. They were among the first northern indigenous peoples to start nation-building. The establishment of the (Nordic) Saami Council in 1956 connected Saami living in Norway, Sweden, and Finland, and Russia since the early-nineteen-nineties. The radical transnational Alta movement against the construction of a hydroelectric power plant spawned a national awakening (even though that particular fight was lost), especially among young Saami and Saami artists, and contributed to the Saami people's self-recognition as a pan-national actor.[24] Similarly, Inuit living in Greenland, Canada, Alaska, and the Russian Far East extended their traditional understanding of homeland by building pan-circumpolar connectivity across national boundaries. The Inuit Circumpolar Conference (now a Council) was founded in 1977.

In the late nineteen-eighties and early nineteen-nineties, northern indigenous peoples took a series of significant steps to build deeper connectivity and cooperation between their organizations. For example, Inuit politically and geographically separated by the Bering Strait began to form new links to the Russian Far East.[25] On the other side of the circumpolar north, the Saami Council and the ICC contributed to the post–cold war Arctic Environmental Protection Strategy—the involvement of indigenous organizations had been neither automatic nor clear at the outset. Then, working with the Russian Association of Indigenous Peoples of the North (RAIPON), they collectively supported the establishment of the Arctic Council in 1996.[26] Although indigenous peoples' organizations were not invited to become founding members of the Arctic Council (like the Arctic states), they were designated Permanent Participants, which gave them rights of active participation and full consultation in the Council.

The status of Arctic Council Permanent Participants is rare, if not unique, for indigenous peoples in global terms. It has opened many doors and created a platform for discussing human development and sustainability face to face with the governments of the Arctic countries. The indigenous peoples, being citizens of states, do not have equal status to the governments of those states, and have much more limited financial resources with which to support participation at the Council's meetings and in its working groups.

All this adds weight to the arguments in favor of greater autonomy through self-determination or self-governance.[27] Achieving the "collective right to decide their own future" has become the main aim of the worldwide movement of indigenous peoples.[28] Arctic indigenous peoples have received increasing recognition of their respective aspirations to nationhood. This is a result of their rich and resilient cultural heritage, vigorous activity, and self-consciousness as nations. Vital to this process of political emergence is the ability of northern peoples and communities to develop "innovative political and legal

24
See Declaration of Murmansk at the 16th Annual Sami Conference in Murmansk, Russia, October 15–18, 1996.

25
Mary Simon, "A Message from Mary Simon, Canadian Ambassador for Circumpolar Affairs," INRIPP – 2, Newsletter (October 2003).

26
See "Declaration on the Establishment of the Arctic Council. Ottawa, 19th day of September 1996."

27
Jerry McBeath, "Changing Forms of Governance in the North," in Heininen and Southcott 2010 (see note 1).

28
"UN International Decade of Indigenous Peoples: Common Objectives and Joint Measures of the Saami Parliaments," a declaration of the meeting of the Saami Parliaments during the spring and fall of 1997.

29
Oran Young and Niels Einarsson, "A Human Development Agenda for the Arctic: Major Findings and Emerging Issues, " in *Arctic Human Development Report* (Akureyri, 2004), p. 237.

30
See Elina Helander-Renvall, "Globalization and Traditional Livelihoods"; Lassi Heininen, "Circumpolar International Relations and Cooperation," in Heininen and Southcott 2010 (see note 1).

31
For more information on environmental and climatic awakening in the Arctic, see Annika Nilsson, "A Changing Arctic Climate: Science and Policy in the Arctic Climate Impact Assessment" *Linköping Studies in Arts and Science,* no. 386 (Linköping, 2007).

32
Mark Nuttall, "Epistemological Conflicts and Cooperation in the Circumpolar North," in Heininen and Southcott 2010 (see note 1); also Chris Paci, "Connecting Circumpolar Environments: Arctic Athabaskan Council and Arctic Council Programmes," in *Circumpolar Connections: Supplementary Proceedings of the 8th Circumpolar Cooperation Conference* (Whitehorse, 2003).

33
Arctic Monitoring and Assessment Programme, "Arctic Pollution" (Oslo, 2002).

arrangements that meet the needs of the residents . . . without rupturing the larger political systems in which the region is embedded."[29]

If nation-building possesses an inherent geopolitical teleology, how far will it go for Arctic indigenous peoples? The ultimate aim of many—to own and control their land and waters —remains, as yet, neither recognized nor implemented. The reality is that the national borders dividing indigenous communities still carry great geopolitical weight. There are, however, more claims on land and water leading to new settlements; the first agreements between the natives, central, and regional governments have already been signed; and there are already the examples of self-governance of Greenland and Nunavut that indicate a clear shift in that direction. Furthermore, internationalization, as well as globalization, has a political logic for Arctic peoples as they attempt to clarify their legal positions and assert their rights to self-determination, sometimes in conflict with the interests of nation-states. In addition, the Arctic is being integrated into the intensifying globalization of world politics.[30]

All this is a northern version of environmental "awakening," started partly by indigenous peoples' organizations and partly by some environmental organizations and a few scientists and scholars. Another key factor is the local or traditional ecological knowledge that comes from indigenous people and other Northerners living close to nature. To be concerned about the state of the environment is very natural or even a way of life, for them, and is also a necessity for survival. In the last decade, there has been an "awakening" in the recognition of climate change, and particularly of global warming, in the High North.

Environmental "Awakening" by Indigenous Peoples[31]

One of the arguments running through this cahier is that indigenous peoples have experimented with a range of technologies—legal, communicative, and environmental —across a range of scales, to exercise their engagement with, and stewardship of, the environment. Consequently in environmental protection, indigenous peoples' organizations have pursued their own agendas. When, for example, the Saami mobilized indigenous support across national borders to resist the damming of the Alta River in Norway, they simultaneously worked in close collaboration with environmental movements and the scientific community.

As a result, cooperation between indigenous peoples and scientific communities has become important in creating new examples of epistemological cooperation for the Arctic.[32] The findings of the Arctic Monitoring Assessment Programme were used to push governments into signing the global Stockholm Convention on Persistent Organic Pollutants.[33] Similarly the

34
Impacts of a Warming Arctic: Arctic Climate Impact Assessment (Cambridge, 2004).

35
See Jan Brösted and Mad. Fægteborg, *Expulsion of the Great People When U.S. Air Force Came to Thule: An Analysis of Colonial Myth and Actual Incidents* (Bergen, 1985), pp. 213–38.

36
Lassi Heininen, "Euroopan pohjoinen 1990-luvulla. Moniulotteisten ja ristiriitaisten intressien alue. Acta Universitatis *Lapponiensis* 21—Arktisen keskuksen tiedotteita" *Arctic Centre Reports* 30 (Rovaniemi, 1999), pp. 242–55.

Arctic Climate Impact Assessment,[34] which brought together a synthesis of scientific evidence and indigenous environmental concern to warn of the effects of climate change on northern traditional livelihoods, has had a considerable impact on governments and intergovernmental organizations.

The strategic military and resource value of northern indigenous homelands have in many cases drawn attention to the divergence of interests between states and their indigenous peoples, and has led to disagreements and even conflicts. More generally, environmental protection of the Arctic has become more complex, sensitive, and international in scope and has put it firmly on foreign policy agendas.[35] Environmental advocacy by international environmental organizations and intergovernmental organizations has inflamed conflicts between indigenous peoples, local entrepreneurs, and national and regional authorities. Trade in marine mammals, minerals, and forest products have all caused deep consternation for indigenous peoples seeking to sustain their traditional livelihoods.[36]

This brings me back to the potential importance of the entire Arctic region in world politics. Here northern indigenous peoples, and their organizations can play an important role if they choose to do so. This raises the broader question as to what counts as environmental action in the spatial politics of indigenous peoples. How and where will the metaphor of the "laboratory" or "workshop" be productively used in climate change issues, be deployed in the future? How will the interplay between traditional and scientific knowledge create new models for action for international cooperation on environmental protection?

Conclusion

The Arctic is an environmental linchpin with a critical role in global environmental issues. It is, however, unclear whether the post–cold war stability and broad international cooperation will continue. One way to support this fruitful process is to recognize indigenous peoples, their livelihoods and agendas, particularly where they deal with the environment. Northern indigenous peoples have not yet been explicit about their interpretation of geopolitics and have not spelled out an agenda for it. They have, however, actively participated in, and to some extent even led, Arctic governance. In other words their perspective on geopolitics is thus far implicit. The question remains whether they will define their geopolitics explicitly and formally.

Context is crucial. Despite the fact that the lands and waters of northern indigenous peoples are mostly divided by national borders, they nevertheless define themselves as nations, and the Arctic as their homeland. They have become credible political actors with stronger voices in their own affairs, and as international actors in international and inter-regional northern cooperation. Consequently they have created a special northern regional dynamics and "connectivity." Given their resilience in the face of these rapid and multi-dimensional changes, is there not every reason to believe that northern indigenous societies can remain viable and thrive in the future?

Contributors

Dr. Michael Bravo
is Head of the Circumpolar History and Public Policy Research Group at the Scott Polar Research Institute, University of Cambridge. He began his career in communications engineering in the Canadian Arctic before moving to the United Kingdom to read the history and philosophy of science for his master's and doctorate. His research group studies Arctic history, governance, and science policy. He contributes to the group through research collaborations and mentoring the next generation of researchers *Writing from the Arctic*. He has played a key role in writing the humanities theme for the recent International Polar Year (2007–2009), the first such "big science" polar event to include explicitly the importance of citizenship as well as the participation of northern peoples and social scientists. Bravo is coeditor of *Narrating the Arctic* (2002) and the author of many scholarly and popular articles in cultural history and the history of science.

Dr. Lassi Heininen
is University Lecturer and Docent at the Faculty of Social Sciences, University of Lapland, Finland. Among his other academic positions are Adjunct Professor at the Frost Center for Canadian Studies, Trent University, Canada, as well as at the Faculty of Geography, University of Oulu, Finland; Visiting Professor at University of Akureyri, Iceland; and Director of the International Summer School in Karelia, Russia. He is also the chairman of the Northern Research Forum. His research fields include International Relations, Geopolitics, Security Studies, Environmental Politics, Political History, and Northern/Arctic Studies. His publications include circa fifty-five scientific articles in international scientific journals and edited volumes, circa eighty scientific articles in Finnish scientific journals and conference proceedings, and twelve scientific monographs.

Katarina Soukup
is an independent producer with almost ten years of experience working as a documentary and multimedia producer with the award-winning, internationally acclaimed Inuit filmmakers Igloolik Isuma Productions, the creative team behind *Atanarjuat (The Fast Runner)* (2000), winner of the Camera d'Or at Cannes 2001. With Isuma, she produced and cowrote the documentary *Kiviaq versus Canada* (2006) with filmmaker Zacharias Kunuk. Soukup founded Catbird Productions in 2006 and has since produced the documentaries *Umiaq Skin Boat* (Official Selection, Hot Docs 2008) and *Kakalak-kuvik—Where the Children Dwell* (2009) by director Jobie Weetaluktuk, as well as *Tusarnituuq! Nagano in the Land of the Inuit* (2009), a documentary by Félix Lajeunesse about the Montreal Symphony Orchestra and conductor Kent Nagano's first ever tour of the Canadian Arctic. She is developing several new projects, including a documentary she will direct on the life of the pioneering Inuit photographer, artist, and historian *Peter Pitseolak.* She holds an MA in Media Studies from Concordia University, Montreal.

Nicola Triscott
is a cultural producer and writer. She is Director of The Arts Catalyst, an interdisciplinary arts commissioning and research organization, which she founded in 1993. Nicola writes and speaks widely in the UK and internationally on the intersections between art, science, technology, and society. Recent essays include "Performative Science in an Age of Specialisation: The Case of Critical Art Ensemble" in *Interfaces of Performance* (Ashgate, 2009), "Once Upon a Space Age: How the Dream Was Lost (and How We Get It Back Again)" in *Human*

Futures: Art in an Age of Uncertainty, (Liverpool, 2008). She is coeditor of *Zero Gravity: A Cultural Users Guide* (London, 2005), and *Malamp: The Occurrence of Deformities in Amphibians—Brandon Ballengee* (London, 2009).

Dr. David Turnbull
is a Senior Research Fellow at the Victorian Eco-Innovation Lab (VEIL) in the Architecture Faculty at Melbourne University. His main research interests are the cross-cultural comparison of ways of knowing, narratives of prehistory, complexity theory, and re-establishing the commons. Recent publications include: *Masons, Tricksters and Cartographers: Comparative Studies in the Sociology of Scientific and Indigenous Knowledge* (London, 2003), "Boundary-Crossings, Cultural Encounters and Knowledge Spaces in Early Australia" in Simon Schaffer et al., eds., *The Brokered World: Go-betweens and Global Intelligence 1770–1820* (Sagamore Beach, 2009), pp. 387–428, "Introduction" in David Turnbull, ed., *Special Issue on the Futures of Indigenous Knowledges, Futures* 41, no.1, (February 2009), pp. 1–5.

Series editors

Dr. Inke Arns
is the artistic director of Hartware MedienKunstVerein (HMKV) in Dortmund, Germany, since 2005. She has worked as an independent curator and writer specializing in media art, Net cultures, and Eastern Europe. Since 1993 she has curated exhibitions in Germany, Great Britain, Hong Kong, Kosovo, Poland, Serbia, Slovenia, and Switzerland. Recent exhibitions: *Irwin: Retroprincip 1983–2003*, 2003; *History Will Repeat Itself*, 2007–08; *Awake Are Only the Spirits*, 2009–10; *Building Memory*, 2010; *Arctic Perspective*, 2010; *inter-cool 3.0: Youth Image Media*, 2010. She lived in Paris (1982–86), studied Slavic studies, Eastern European studies,

political science, and art history in Berlin and Amsterdam (1988–96) and has held teaching positions at universities and art academies in Berlin, Leipzig, Rotterdam, Zurich, and Dortmund. She has lectured and published internationally.

Matthew Biederman
is an artist living in Montreal, Canada, and the director of C-TASC. He has been performing, installing, and exhibiting artworks which explore themes of perception, media saturation, and data systems since the mid-nineties. Biederman was the recipient of the Bay Area Artist Award in Video by New Langton Arts in 1999, and the First Prize in the Visual Arts category of Slovenia's Break21 festival. His work has been exhibited in the USA, South America, and Europe in a variety of festivals and venues.

Marko Peljhan
is a conceptual artist and a theater and radio director by profession. He is the founder and director of the arts and technology organization Projekt Atol, Ljubljana, Slovenia, and the codirector of the University of California's Institute for Research in the Arts, Santa Barbara. Peljhan worked on the Makrolab project that focuses on telecommunications, migrations, and weather systems research from 1997–2007, and the Interpolar Transnational Art Science Constellation during the International Polar Year 2006–09. He is the recipient of many prizes, including the Golden Nica at Ars Electronica (with Carsten Nicolai) in 2000 and the UNESCO Digital Media Prize in 2004. He holds an appointment with the Department of Art and the Media Arts & Technology graduate program at the University of California Santa Barbara.

This publication is published in conjunction with the project *Arctic Perspective—Third Culture*

arcticperspective.org

Editors
Michael Bravo
Nicola Triscott

Series editors
Inke Arns
Matthew Biederman
Marko Peljhan
Nicola Triscott

Proofreading
Miranda Pope
Geoffrey Garrison

Cover design
PKMB

Production
Nadine Schmidt,
Hatje Cantz

Printing and binding
fgb freiburger graphische betriebe

Paper
Munken print, 100 g/m²;
Hello gloss, 135 g/m²

© 2011 Hatje Cantz Verlag, Ostfildern; Arctic Perspective Initiative; editors and authors

© 2011 for the reproduced works by
pp. 4–5 Pudlo Pudlat's painting reproduced with the permission of Dorset Fine Arts
p. 8 Courtesy of DNV
p. 43 Scott Polar Research Institute, University of Cambridge
p. 47 National Geographic: Image Collection
p. 79 *Tupaia's Chart* reproduced with the permission of the British Library Board
p. 79 *Tupaia's Chart Reconstructed* reproduced with permission of the Journal of Polynesian Studies
p. 98 Glenbow Museum

Every effort has been made to trace copyright holders. However, if any have been overlooked inadvertently, HMKV will be pleased to discuss necessary arrangements at the first opportunity.

Katarina Soukup's essay is reproduced by permission of the Canadian Journal of Communications.

Published by
Hatje Cantz Verlag
Zeppelinstrasse 32
73760 Ostfildern
Germany
Tel. +49 711 4405-200
Fax +49 711 4405-220

www.hatjecantz.com

Hatje Cantz books are available internationally at selected bookstores. For more information about our distribution partners, please visit our website.

ISBN 978-3-7757-2681-8

Printed in Germany

Thanks to
The authors
Simon Anderson
Claudio Aporta
Martin Bryant
Klaus Dodds
John MacDonald
Jackie Price
Bryan Lintott
Simon Schaffer
Nancy Wachowich

HMKV
Dr. Inke Arns, Andrea Eichardt, Frauke Hoffschulte, Susanne Ackers
    Projekt Atol
Andrej Bizjak, Miha Bratina, Marko Gabrijelčič, Barbara Hribar, Marko Peljhan, Sašo Podgoršek, Samo Stopar, Nejc Trost
    Lorna
Páll Thayer, Margrét Elísabet Ólafsdóttir
    C-TASC
Matthew Biederman
    The Arts Catalyst
Rob La Frenais, Gillean Dickie, Jo Fells, Shiraz Ksaiba

Arctic Perspective Initiative

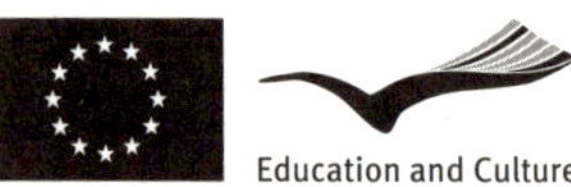

With the support of the Culture Programme of the European Union

Culture Programme

This project has been funded with support from the European Commission. This publication reflects the views only of the authors, and the Commission cannot be held responsible for any use which may be made of the information contained therein.

Funded by

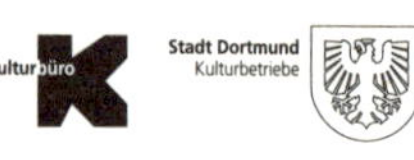

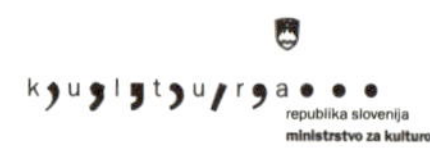

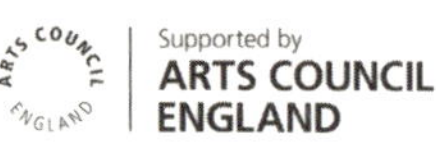

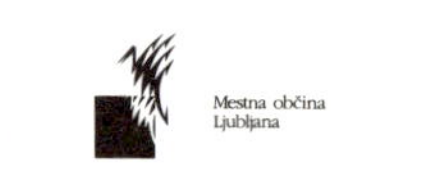

Front cover
Herve Paniaq, Foxe Basin, August 2009. Photo: API
Back cover
Zacharias Kunuk and crew, Foxe Basin, August 2009. Photo: API

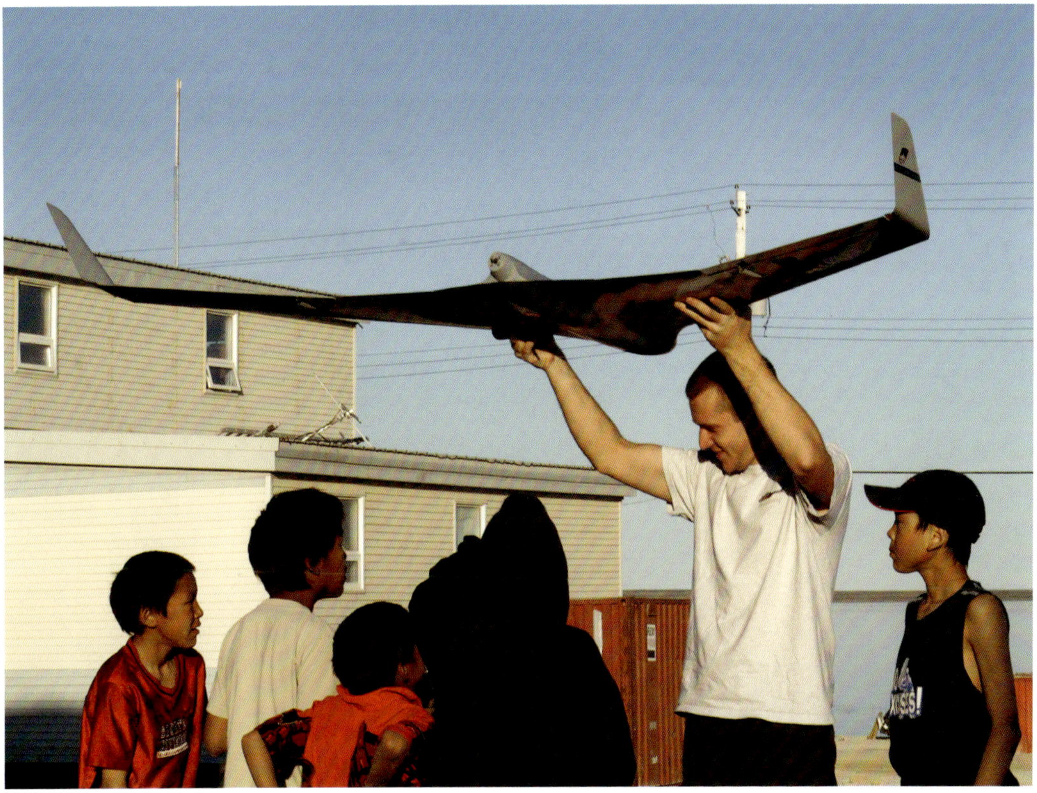

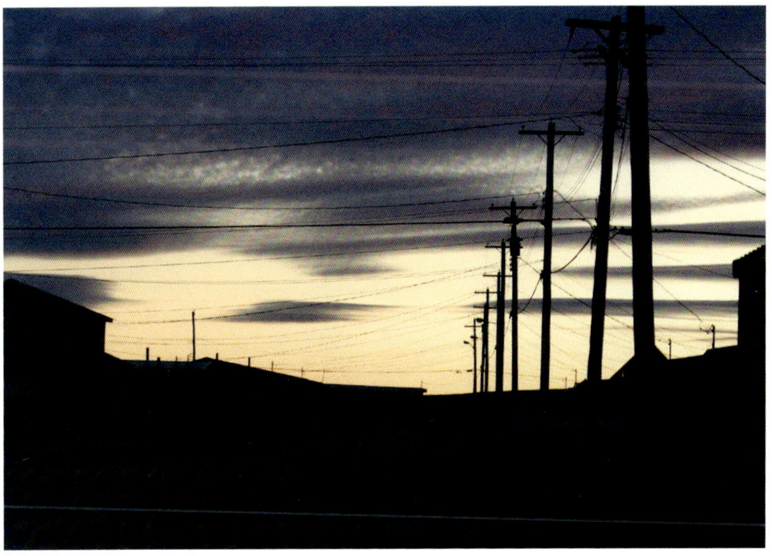

Nejc Trošt performing preflight checks of the Bramor UAS in Igloolik, 2009.
Photo: Matthew Biederman

Igloolik during the midnight sun, 2009.
Photo: Matthew Biederman

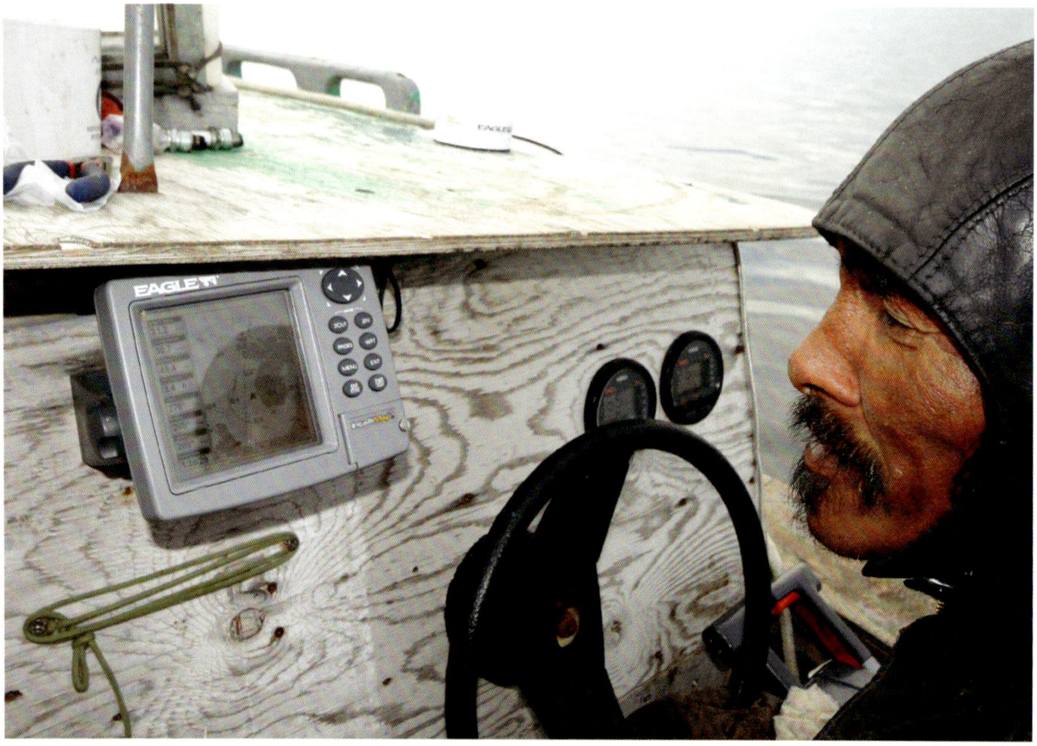

Harry Ikerapik Ittuksarjuat navigates Foxe Basin with the assistance of an onboard GPS system, 2009. Photo: API

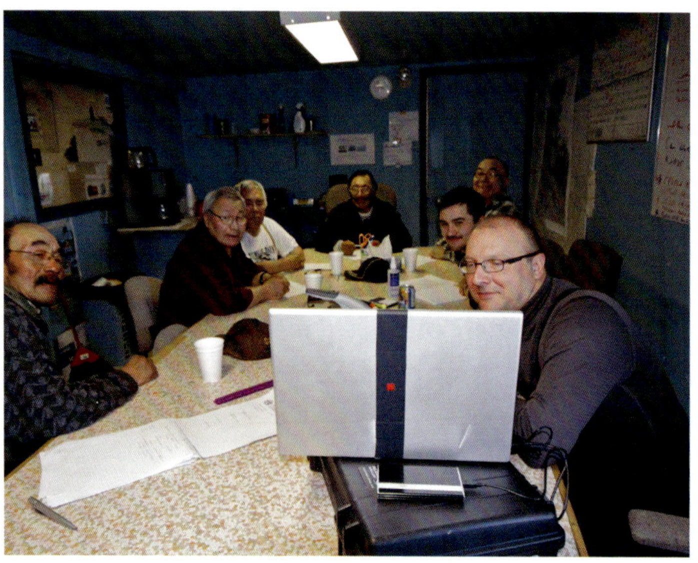

API discussing the Kallitaq design with the members of the Pond Inlet HTO, 2010. Photo: Matthew Biederman

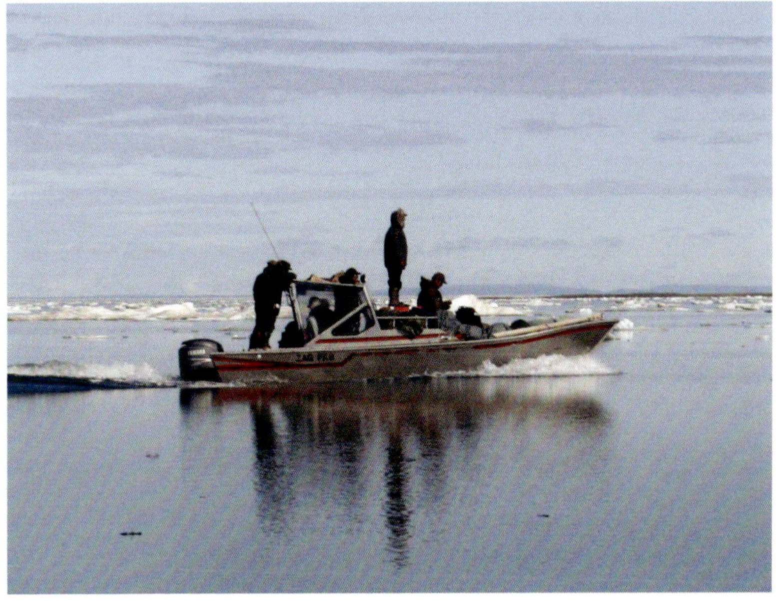

Looking for a way through the sea ice. Zacharias Kunuk and crew,
Foxe Basin, 2009. Photo: API

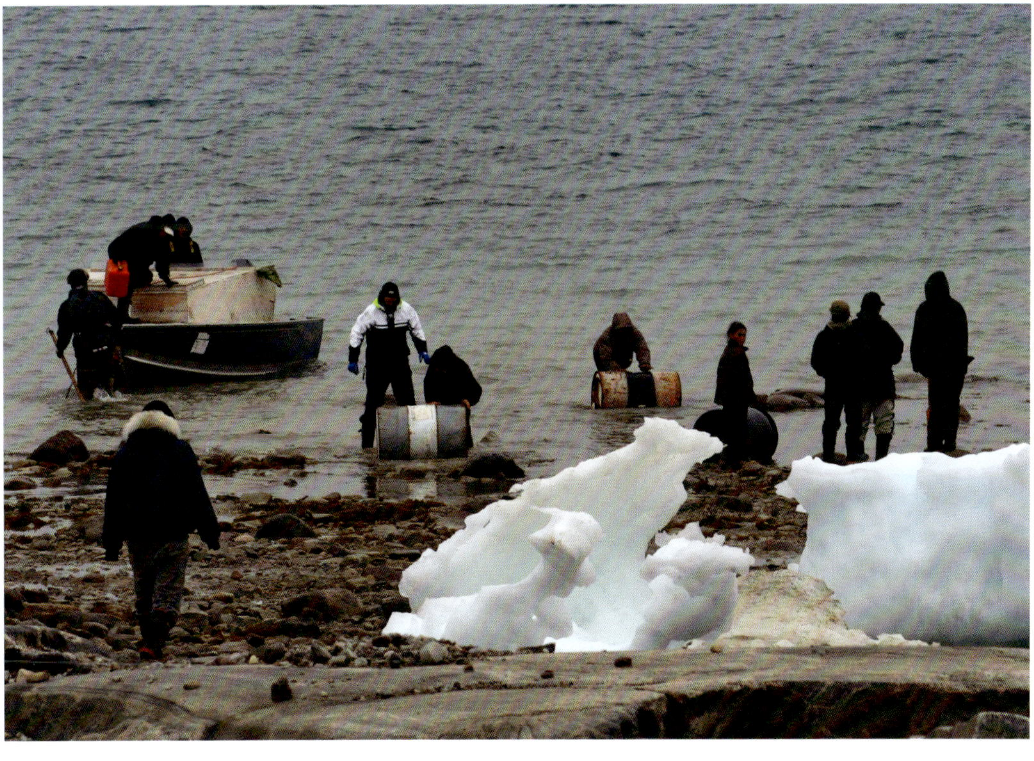

Unloading fuel to cache at Maniqtuuk Island for the return to Ikpik, Foxe Basin, 2009.
Photo: Matthew Biederman

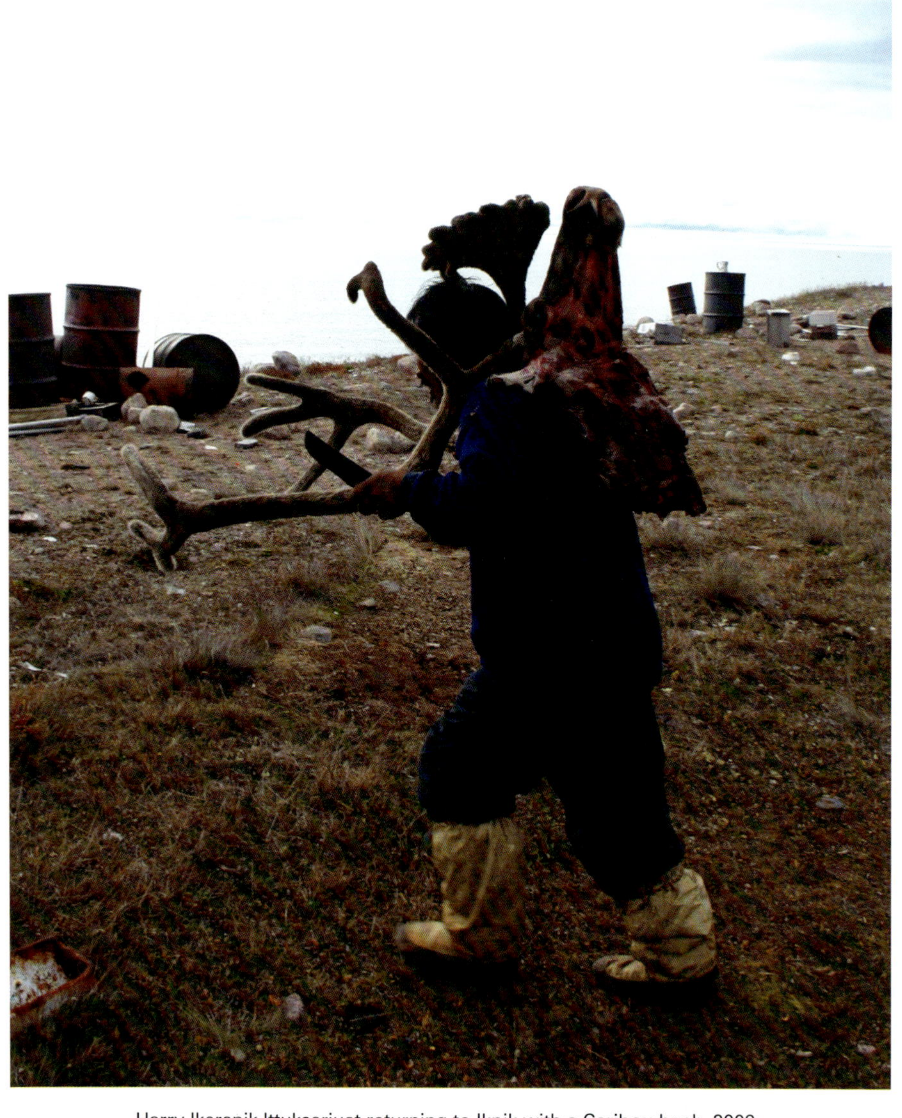

Harry Ikerapik Ittuksarjuat returning to Ikpik with a Caribou buck, 2009.
Photo: Nejc Trošt

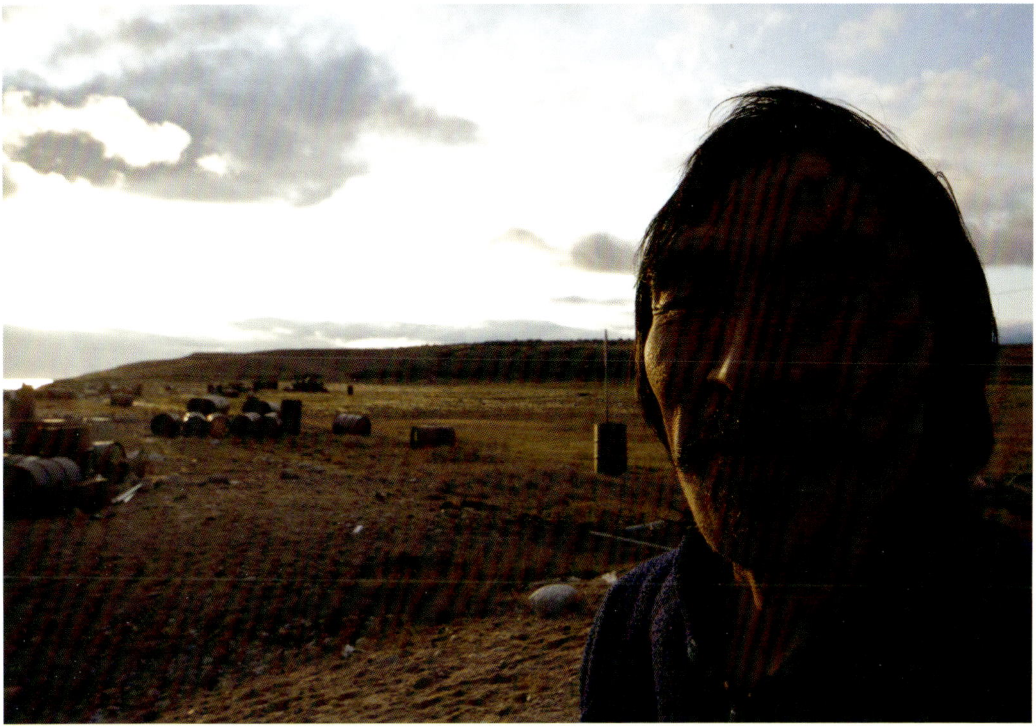

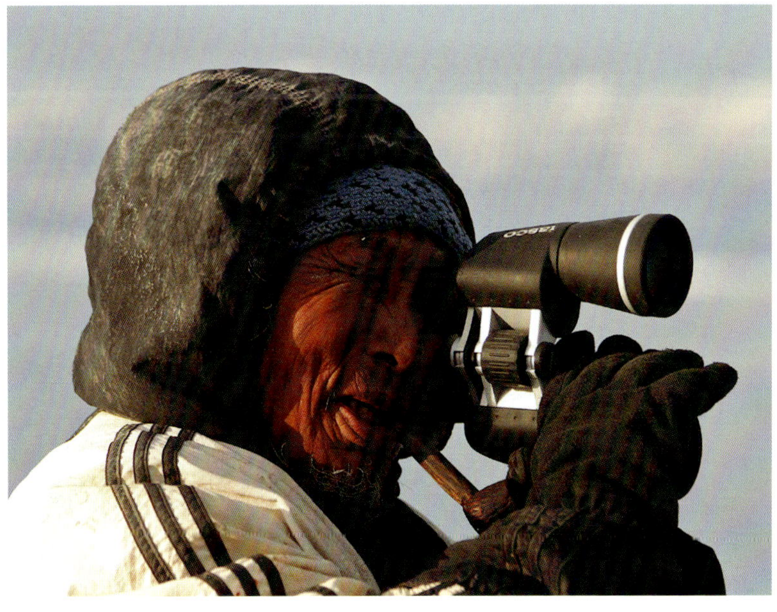

Harry Ikerapik Ittuksarjuat at Ikpik settlement after returning there for the first time in approximately twenty years. Harry spent several years with his parents, a few other families, and Father Fournier during his youth. 2009. Photo: Marko Peljhan

Herve Paniaq searches for holes in the pack ice while navigating in Foxe Basin, August 2009. Photo: API

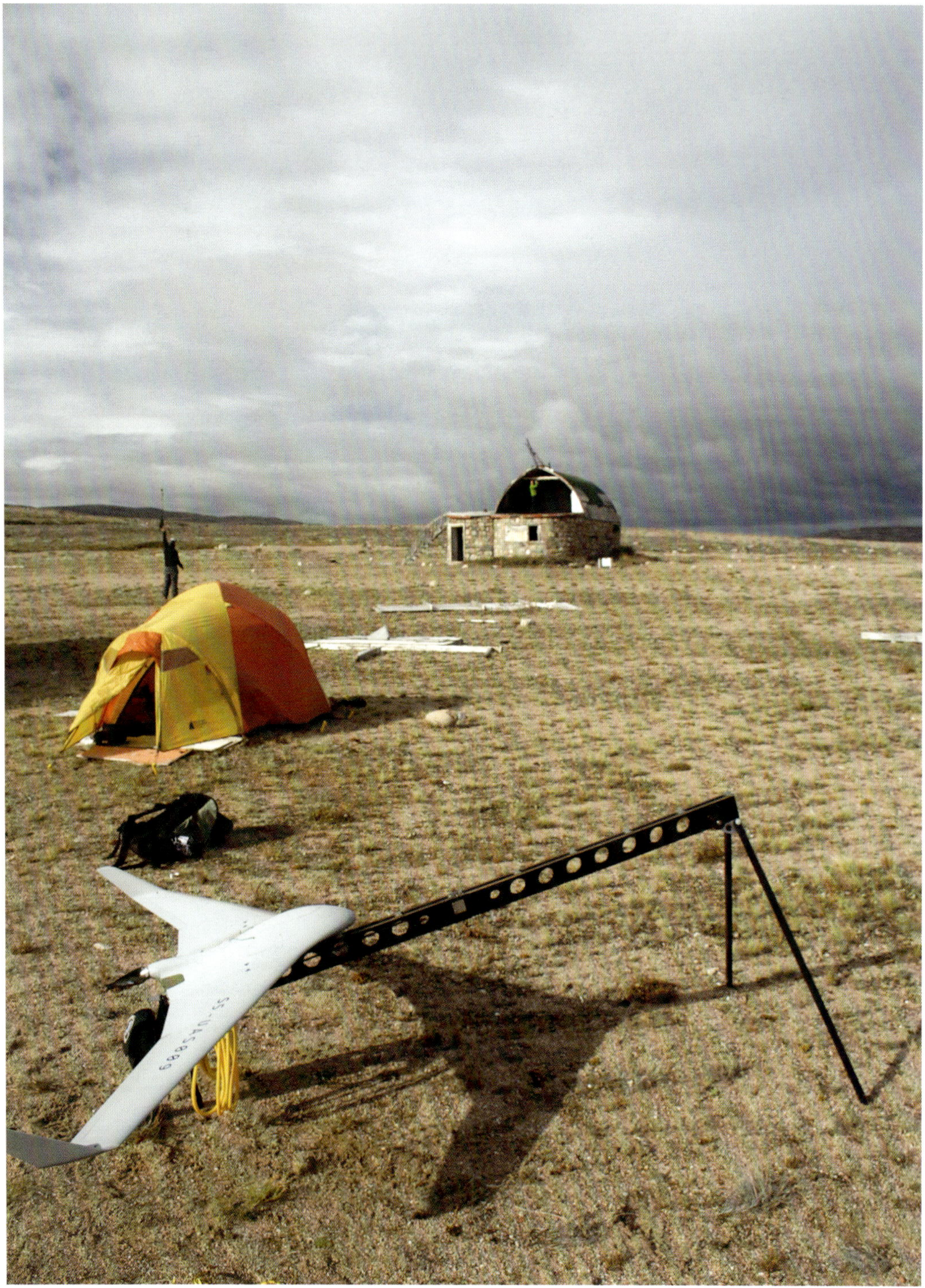

Camp at Ikpik. Bramor UAS in foreground with API's sleeping tent behind. In the distance, Marko and Matthew hang an antenna from the old church of Ikpik, 2009. Photo: API

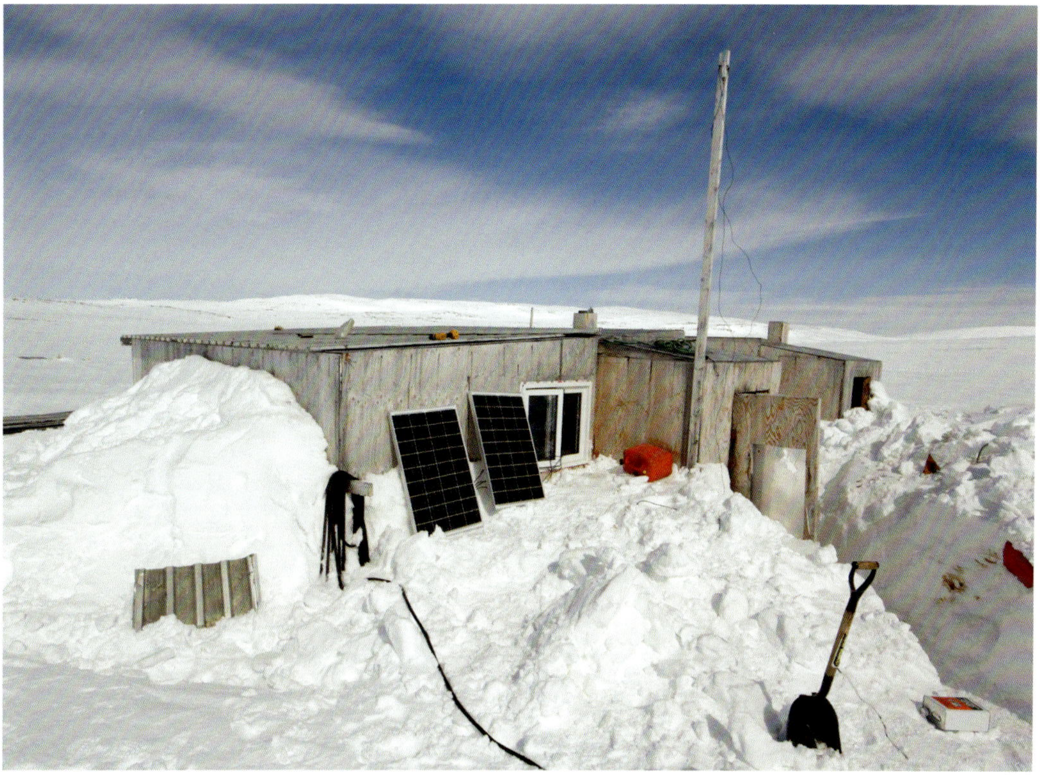

Zacharius Kunuk's camp at Siuraarjuk. Solar panels connected to API's Isagutaq power system are used to power the cabin and supply electricity for the first satelitte video link to London on the ocassion of the "Autonomy and Technology in the North" panel at Canada House, 2010. Photo: Matthew Biederman

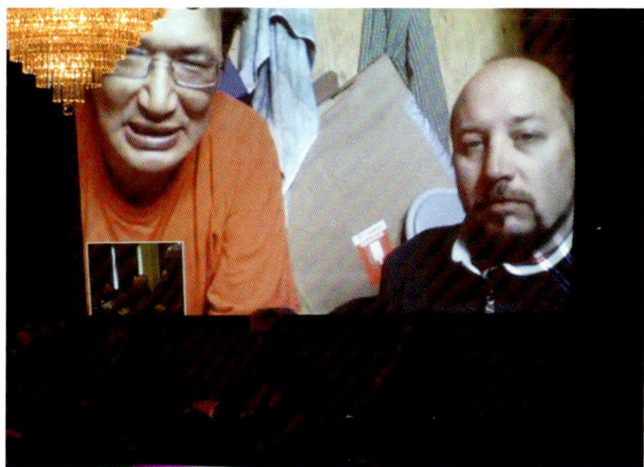

Zacharias Kunuk and Matthew Biederman appear on screen live via satellite connection from Siuraajuk, NU, to Canada House, London, UK, during the Autonomy and Technology in the North panel discussion, 2010. Photo: Paul Glen

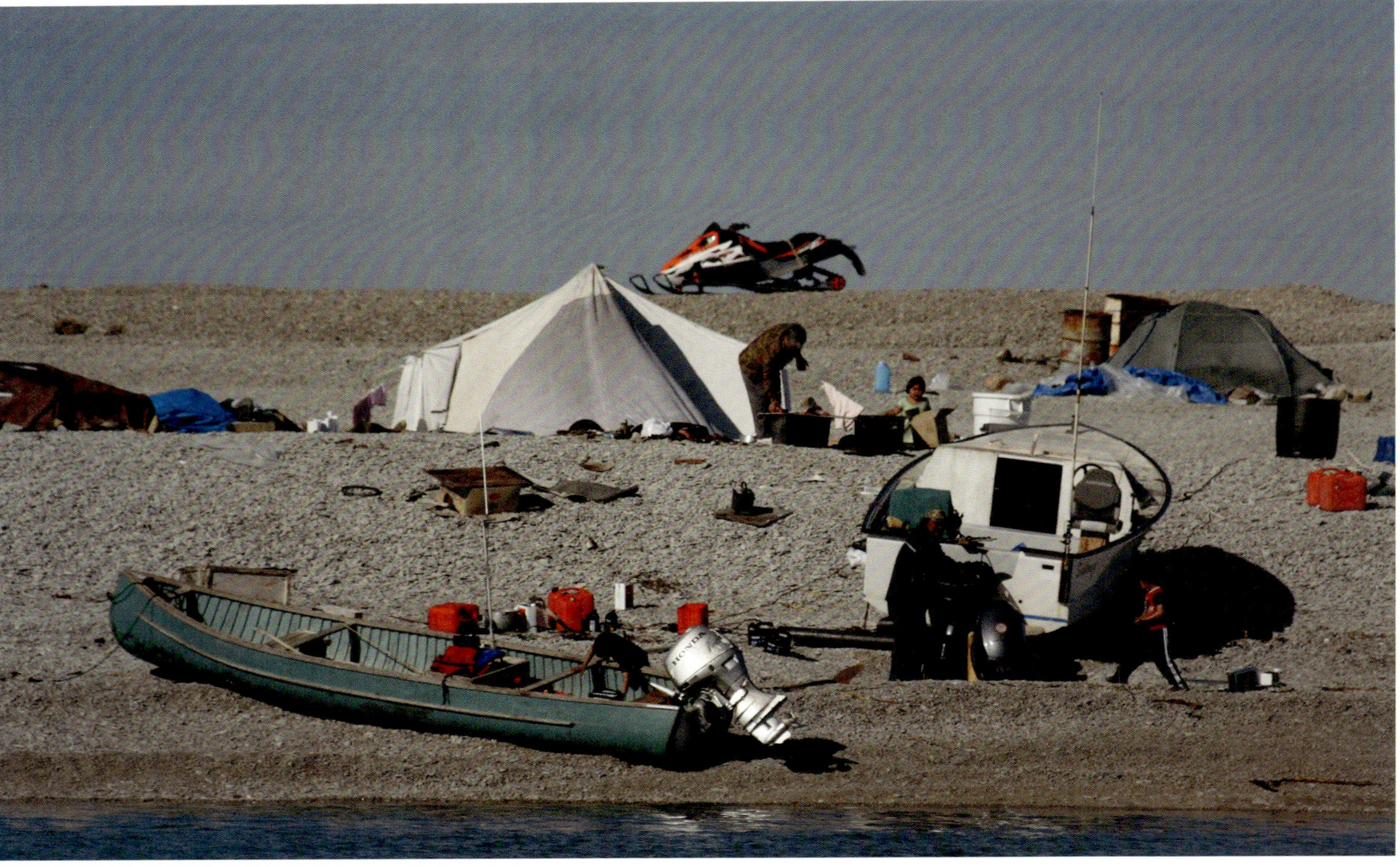

Temporary camp in Turton Bay, Igloolik Island, Foxe Basin, 2009. Photo: API